Basic Sobriety:
Shambhala Buddhism and the Twelve Steps

Basic Sobriety

Basic Sobriety:
Shambhala Buddhism and the Twelve Steps

Eric Rainbeau

Empedrado Street Press
2016

Basic Sobriety

The Twelve Steps and brief excerpts from *Alcoholics Anonymous* and *Twelve Steps and Twelve Traditions* are reprinted with permission of Alcoholics Anonymous World Services, Inc. ("A.A.W.S.") Permission to reprint these excerpts does not mean that A.A.W.S. has reviewed or approved the contents of this publication, or that A.A.W.S. necessarily agrees with the views expressed herein. A.A. is a program of recovery from alcoholism only – use of these excerpts in connection with programs and activities which are patterned after A.A., but which address other problems, or in any other non A.A. context, does not imply otherwise. Additionally, while A.A. is a spiritual program, A.A. is not a religious program. Thus, A.A. is not affiliated or allied with any sect, denomination, or specific religious belief.

Excerpts from *It works, How and Why and Narcotics Anonymous* are reprinted by permission of NA World Services, Inc. All rights reserved.

Kabat-Zinn, Jon. *Full Catastrophe Living: Using the Wisdom of Your Body and Mind to Face Stress, Pain, and Illness*. New York, NY: Delacorte, 1990.
Hanh, Nhat. *Zen Keys*. New York: Doubleday, 1995.
Trungpa, C., & Gimian, C. R. (1984). *Shambhala: The sacred path of the warrior*. Boulder, Colo: Shambhala.
Trungpa, C. (1985). *Journey without goal: The tantric wisdom of the Buddha*. Boston: Shambhala.
Trungpa, C. (1991). *The heart of the Buddha*. Boston: Shambhala.
Hayward, Jeremy W. *Warrior-King of Shambhala: Remembering Chogyam Trungpa*, Boston: Wisdom Publications, 2008
C., Chuck. *A New Pair of Glasses*. Irvine, CA: New-Look Pub. 1984.
Shantideva, *The Way of the Bodhisattca: A Translation of the Bodhicharyavatara*. Boston: Shambhala, 1997.

First Printing: Impermanent Edition 2016

ISBN 978-1-365-46764-6

Empedrado Street Press
3218 Empedrado Street Press
Tampa, FL 33629

www.basicsobriety.com

Ordering Information: Trade bookstores, wholesalers and special groups special discounts are available on quantity purchases. Please contact Eric Rainbeau by email at basicsobriety@gmail.com

To my wife and children

I am humbled by your pressence in my life

Table of Contents

Basic Sobriety

Step Zero

But Meditation is Step 11

Meditation is a powerful tool. Throughout this book, I will be discussing the practice of meditation. I suggest you begin a meditation practice as quickly as you can and in whatever form you can. If at the beginning it is merely 5 minutes a day, and 3 of those minutes are walking meditation, then begin there. You do not need to wait until you reach Step Eleven to say, "Ok now I am going to start meditating." Step Eleven is where the founders of Alcoholics Anonymous placed meditation and I believe they had a very good reason for doing so, which I will elucidate in the chapter on Step Eleven. However, in those early days of AA the Steps were also done in a matter of hours. Chances are you reached Step Eleven within days of getting sober, and not months or years like we may hear of today. If it takes you eleven months to reach Step Eleven, chances are you will tell yourself that meditation is hard and that you've gotten along fine without it.

Start meditating as soon as you can. Finding a meditation center and people to meditate with helps because having people sitting around you is both a great inspiration and a deterrent to giving up a few minutes in. This is the same as getting sober alone. Maybe we could do it alone but fellowship and companionship on the path of recovery make it a lot easier.

So yes, the founders put meditation at Step Eleven but I believe we can begin right at Step One. When we come to Step Eleven, then our meditation will take on a new and richer dimension.

The Shambhala Path of Warriorship is a graduated path of education developed by Chogyam Trungpa Rinpoche that consists of retreat weekends and weekly classes. The Path of Warriorship gives us tools to help us with the Steps along the way, whether we do the classes before we get sober or after we have been sober for decades.

Basic Sobriety

Just as the Twelve Steps are not a one and done proposition, neither is the Path of Warriorship. Taking all the classes, while providing us with wonderful tools and knowledge, is not a cure for the disease of addiction. We need to work these principles in all our affairs for our own basic sanity to grow and flourish.

If you do partake in the Way of Shambhala classes and retreats, there is a good chance they will not coincide with your progress through the steps. Do not worry. Since we need to continually practice all the Steps and principles, the ideas, concepts and practices that we learn through the levels will be further support in our recovery. They will strengthen your spiritual experience wherever you are along your path. By practicing a spiritual path, even a non-denominational one, we are giving ourselves the best chance for sobriety. When we are peaceful and serene there is nothing for drugs and alcohol to fix.

Even if you never set foot in a Shambhala center or take a class on meditation, what I present here can serve as tools to look at the world and the Steps from a new perspective. The ideas are rooted in very ancient teachings. What is presented in the pages that follow is only the tip of the iceberg. How deep you want to go is up to you. Not all the ideas presented here will be found in the Path of Warriorship classes. The Path of Warriorship was where I built my foundation of meditation and spirituality. Some of my tools came from the rooms of recovery; the other tools came from the shrine room. I hope you will find some new tools to aid your recovery.

They have worked for me and I hope they will help you too.

Preface

Two weeks ago, an Acharya (a senior teacher in the Shambhala lineage) asked me how I came to be standing in front of her at Shambhala Mountain Center in Colorado.

My response was "Kicking and screaming, but let me explain."

Here is a slightly longer version of that explanation:

Shortly after getting sober, sitting in the rooms, I realized what most of us realize: "They mention God a lot!" Well really, they mention having a "Higher Power" a great deal. In all matters religious, I had a head full of misplaced ideas, lots of prejudices, and no concept of any form of a working relationship with a power greater than myself. I had been that power most of my life and the farther I went down the alcoholic trail, the more disastrous the results.

Ignorant and naïve, I did not understand that the majority of the hardships I had gone through were related to the fact that I drank the majority of the time--that my hardships were of my own making. Alcohol finally brought me to the position where I was about to lose all the things I had struggled to regain after 16 months of unemployment, an unemployment which at the time I conveniently blamed on the recession, but now know differently. I was working, had my own place again, and a new woman had entered my life. I was frantically trying to keep the sand castle I had managed to rebuild from being ripped apart in the storm of my continued drinking. It was not looking good and the barometer was falling. All the "I'll quit when's" had started to fade into the distance and I could not stop drinking. Worse, the new woman in my life did not drink. Sure, I had lost the previous two significant women in my life to drinking, but I lied to myself that they were the cause of my drinking; my drinking was not the cause of their leaving.

I could self-reason and diagnose that I did not have a drinking problem or if I did it was in the past. You know, when times had been rough I "probably drank more often than I should have." Unfortunately then, when everything was looking up again, I continued to drink a case of beer or more each evening. I had started calling in sick again, as I was too hungover or drunk from the night before to come to work or get out of bed. The writing on the wall was becoming clear; the end was drawing near.

Worst of all was that while I was with this new woman, I did not drink. As our dates began to gather frequency and duration, the two sides of my life became very distinctly apparent. On those days we were together I was able to not drink. Strangely, life was actually enjoyable without a drink, or twenty. The problem was I could only seem to manage that while we were together. Once our dates ended and I went back to my place, I would start drinking before I even made it to the front door.

Two divorces and three children, overdrawn bank accounts, going from making $100k a year in a cute little artsy town outside New York City to a one-room "cottage" with no kitchen for four people in a redneck carney town, that desire to kill myself or run away to the Peace Corps, no friends, no family, and a career that held so much promise but no fruition, had not been enough to introduce me to desperation or even to the idea that I should not drink. Surely that should have been enough, but I could not fathom a life without drinking. Even when I didn't want to drink, I found myself drinking. I could not seem to not drink.

The more I began to fall in love with the woman I spent my sober days with, the more I began to despise who I was on the days I was not sober. This began a very powerful and increasing downward spiral of despair and depression that was hidden even further with greater and greater amounts of beer and whiskey. This was my true introduction to and realization of the "incomprehensible demoralization" that few would know. Each day I awoke with the resolve to not drink and failed miserably each evening. This seemed worse than the terror of waking up those unemployed mornings not knowing if I had enough money or alcohol to get drunk that day.

Now each day was progressively getting worse and I could not see a way out. I was all fear and no hope the day we began a 21-day meditation challenge.

Now, don't go thinking that I started that and never drank again. Not so but one day something odd did happen. We began the challenge on a long weekend together, so we had 3 or 4 days of listening to the recordings, doing the meditations and then discussing the experience. When I went home I had the heartfelt intention of staying sober--at least sober long enough to do the meditation before we talked that evening. I didn't quite make it that far and started drinking before the thought hit me that she might ask about that day's mediation. So I arranged a cushion and two more beers within arm's reach, and then hit play on the recording. Ten minutes and 3 empty beers later, I opened my eyes and for the first time clearly saw what the root of my problem was. There I sat on the floor, listening to this calm voice, and I continued to crack beer after beer. This was drinking because of me and no one else. Drinking always remained, regardless of all the other pieces and parts of my life. I needed to stop drinking or I would just continue to play the same movie over and over again. I redoubled my efforts to get through a day without getting drunk, trying to further rein in the beast, and each morning waking up with a pile of empty cans and bottles. Unsuccessful, the demoralization grew larger and larger.

"Honey, I think I have a drinking problem." I one day mustered the courage to confess. I didn't know what to expect. She had not had a drink in years and here I was unable to stay sober 15 minutes on my own. I was lost and needed help. Would she tell me to leave? I had hid my drinking from her for almost 4 months, telling innumerable lies to cover it up. "I am really scared about going home because I can't be there without getting drunk." She recommended I go to AA, find a meeting in a church, and see what happened from there. She had a friend whom it had worked for, so it might work for me, although I doubted it

That night I found myself in a dark corner of a church parking lot, crying my eyes out. There was no one left to call, no one left who would save me. I knew going home was another night of drinking myself to oblivion and I could not do it again. Terrified, I realized that I had no idea how not to drink. Scared, shaking and confused, I followed some people into a huge room.

So began my life in AA.

If He Were Sought

A few months into my life in AA, I found myself struggling with the Third Step, "Made a decision to turn our will and our lives over to the care of God as we understood him" (Big Book of AA). There was that God word and I really wanted nothing much to do with the Christian God that most of the folks around here were talking about. It was not the decision part but just flat-out who is this God person I was supposed to be turning my will over to? In my youth, religion was not a part of our daily life. I grew up in a somewhat Jewish household, Jewish father and agnostic mother, getting bar mitzvahed at 13 and sent to Catholic high school at 14. During college I "studied" Buddhism and Taoism, only to have all religious teachings washed away by an ocean of Budweiser and Jack Daniels. I got a first class education in suffering, though. I was thoroughly lost.

So I began at the beginning, finding a Jewish synagogue and returning to services. They were enjoyable, a Jewish Indigo Girls concert every Friday evening. The Rabbi had some wonderful things to say but they did not resonate deeply enough to foster faith or belief. Sure, it was wonderful for all of them, and I wished I could believe as they did, but alas there was still that emptiness within me. I prayed each morning and night and throughout the day as my sponsor told me to. I prayed because he told me to pray. I believed because my sponsor believed. Then one day at the library I wandered into the religion section and picked up a book on Buddhism that seemed nice, which led to another book, and another. I like to read.

The third book was a compilation of different Buddhist writers. I was adrift in this thing called Buddhism, still all in my head and trying to get beyond the one concept that I always got lost in, "Life is Suffering". Yep, I had that one down. Yet, in meeting after meeting I saw people who seemed happy. I knew that not all of them believed in the traditional God on high concept. Even the old guy who recently celebrated 50 years of sobriety--sprinkled within his "All God. Total God. 24-7 God." was the idea that it was not the church's God but merely a God of his own understanding that was his anchor during his decades of sobriety. I was told that each of them rose above it, alcoholism and suffering, through the ABCs which appear on page 60 of the Big Book of Alcoholics Anonymous, which states "C. God could and would if he was sought." So my seeking continued and in the universe's wisdom I came upon this compilation of short, pithy Buddhist writings and it was sitting in my bag one weekend when my girlfriend and I were attending a wedding in the middle of nowhere. While I slept, my bored girlfriend saw the book. She opened to a page and started reading. The short piece she opened to was written by someone named Pema Chodron and it struck a chord, or rather it played a whole symphony, as my girlfriend found piece after piece by Pema. My girlfriend did not tell me about her experience when I awoke later that morning for breakfast. Later in the week, I stopped by a bookstore and Pema's little yellow book seemed to jump into my hand. Thinking my girlfriend might enjoy a female writer, I bought it and a few other books. I was quite surprised by her reaction--"Pema is a woman!"-- which then began her searching for more information about who this person was that struck her so deeply.

A half hour on the Internet and my girlfriend knew a bit more about who this Pema person was.

More research unveiled Pema's connection to the Shambhala lineage and that there was a Shambhala center in the next city, about 30 minutes away across the bay. One Sunday evening we went for an open house, then another, and another. When they offered the "Level 1" weekend, we signed up. My girlfriend was all excited, but I was terrified. Sure, two twenty minute sits in an evening were bearable, but a whole weekend alone in my own head! You must be crazy. I must be crazy. In the rooms there is a saying, "An alcoholic alone in their own head is a dangerous place to be," and you expect me to do it for two days? The day before the retreat, in a panic, I called one of the teachers. He explained that many people actually found retreats to be an enjoyable experience, finding their minds to be more spacious afterwards (whatever that meant). With skepticism and reluctance, I went to the weekend.

It was painful yet strangely enjoyable. I did not go insane-- well, at least not more insane than I already was (thank you Step Two). We signed up for the next level and the one after that. During that time we continued to go to the weekend evening gatherings and the morning sitting sessions when we could. The concept of a recovery group began to pop up around the center and the idea slowly gained traction. I was extremely interested in this but obstacles kept coming up to prevent my involvement in the group. As fate would have it, once the decision to go forward with the group was made it was at a bad time, on a bad night for me and I resigned myself to let it slip through my fingers. The center turned to another member who had much longer sobriety than I did for leadership of the group. He had a meeting or two getting the format developed, listening to the desires of the sangha, and the whole thing began without me.

The gentleman who was leading the group enjoyed the recovery meeting at the center, but his home group also met that night and he missed going there. Reluctant to miss another week at his home group, he asked if I could cover him at the meeting one night. I rearranged some things in my schedule so that I could be available and the original organizer returned to his home group. I have to admit I hoped he would ask. YES! A year and change sober and even though I had gone through the steps I was still struggling with the whole higher power thing. This was exactly what I believed I needed. Little did I know the effect the group would have on my entire life.

Another senior sangha member was there each week but she did not have official Twelve Step experience, so the two of us would manage to "run" the meeting each week. I loved each week's meeting. New people would come to the center, people of all sorts and with all sorts of issues. Many of them were from other lineages and many identified with different aspects of the "ism". One day the senior sangha member announced she was moving and I was the one left running the meeting each week. Now, when newcomers had questions, I was the one people looked to for answers, which I did my best to answer. One day Shambhala Guide training was posted on the bulletin board at our center. The description was exactly what I was looking for, to be able to learn meditation instruction and more importantly, about the history, teachings and lineage of Shambhala.

But of course there were prerequisites.

This is where everything changed. We had just finished level three. The prerequisites were that you needed to finish all five levels and the Everyday Life series, do a week long sitting and meditate an hour a day. Whereas before I was reluctant, now I dove right in. Suddenly my path had direction. There was purpose and meaning. I could carry the message, giving freely what had been feely been given to me. Of course, I had to first have something to give away. I signed up for the training, committed to my sponsor that I would do the one hour a day meditation and signed up for all the prerequisites. Game on.

It is at this point, the daily one hour of meditation, that everything changed. Discipline not only brought joy; it brought the beginning of faith: faith in the path, faith in meditation, and faith in the Shambhala teachings. By the time the Guide training came about, it seemed everything had already changed. Whatever was going to happen that weekend, whether I "passed or failed" as a guide, the results of a daily meditation practice were starting to show. More importantly, when I exclaimed to my wife, "Whew, at last I can stop meditating an hour a day," she responded, "No, you can't. You've changed and we ALL like this version of you better."

I felt like Charlie Brown right after Lucy pulls the football out from in front of him.

Luckily for all, the homework for the class was to continue meditating an hour a day, so I did not have much of a choice anyway. Either way, I was firmly on the path now. A few twenty-four hours have gone by since then and almost every Thursday evening I've been at the center leading or supporting the Heart of Recovery group, and almost everything in my life has changed.

After the interview with the Acharya, I found myself sitting on a hillside beneath a pine tree. The valley spread before me. The Rocky Mountains made a wonderful backdrop for the shrine tent across the way. Years ago I was peering over the edge into the abyss; now I was peering into a mountain valley, in the middle of a two-week retreat, daily emails to my wife and daughters, a text each day to my sponsor and I was there all because I was sober.

Whatever Form You Relate To

To create my sobriety I have walked with one foot in AA and the other following the Shambhala path. Each time I pick up a book, take a class, or watch a talk, I inevitably jot down a step that relates to the subject at hand. It always seems to fit together. The following chapters are an exploration about how the Shambhala Path of the Warrior teachings works with the program of Alcoholics Anonymous, because for me-- they came together like a zipper, interlocking to create a path that has lead to a solid sobriety. I believe that the two paths joined together can work for others as well.

There are a number of wonderful dharma recovery books, books about the Shambhala teachings, Buddhist books and recovery books out in the world today. This is not a definitive study on any of those subjects. Other dharma recovery books inevitably speak the language of their lineage. What I aspire to show is the bridge between the Twelve Steps and the Shambhala path that I have followed. The following chapters will illustrate that bridge from the principles of the steps to the Shambhala path of Warriorship, the path of the four dignities.

"If you want what we have to offer, and are willing to make the effort to get it, then you are ready to take certain steps. *These are the principles* that made our recovery possible" (NA Basic Text).

There are many versions of the principles of recovery, much like there are many versions of the Ten Commandments. As a working point I start with the AA principles, then bring it to the current path of Shambhala Warriorship of the four dignities as taught today. The program of AA and the path of Shambhala Buddhism are merely tools. Using these tools, I believe we can create a full program of recovery--a full, complete, whole person, regardless of our addiction or place on the path.

While my experience has been primarily with the program and meetings of Alcoholics Anonymous, I hope that all who share the disease of addiction can relate to the stories told in this book and my journey. When I use the word alcoholic or refer to drinking, I do not mean to exclude any of the other "isms". Given the right causes and conditions, I can be addicted to almost anything and while alcohol may have been the chief offender, I know that I have issues with drugs, sex, co-dependency and food to name a few.

By my early twenties I already knew how I had found the drug of my choice in alcohol. Then, as most of us do, we develop a particular "high" we are chasing. Other substances, even other forms of alcohol, provided different highs, which never felt as satisfying as the one I knew and loved. Either way, self-knowledge of knowing my addictive nature kept me from other dry goods that would have quickened my descent into madness. I have watched other issues crawl out from the woodwork once I put down the bottle. They were not new ones, just hidden behind the bottle. My understanding of others is through relating to my own deeper issues on all manners of addiction, including the big bad Buddhist one of "addiction to self."

I do hope that all will benefit from this book, regardless of what form of addiction you relate to or if you care for someone who suffers or you simply want to learn some tools for letting go of some less than healthy habits. This is not meant to be a standalone method of recovery. I am not out to rewrite the Big Book of Alcoholics Anonymous or Narcotics Anonymous' Basic Text, or tell you that this alone can get or keep you sober. As a friend says, "We cannot get anyone sober, nor can we get anyone drunk." I have needed the AA program of the Twelve Steps and the AA fellowship tremendously to get me to this point. I still go to multiple meetings a week, call my sponsor on an almost daily basis, and see him and the guys I sponsor once a week if our schedules allow. If you suffer please utilize whichever program you need, as well as members of the medical community. The Big Book tells us that we need to be "willing to go to any lengths" for our recovery, so use every method and means possible to maintain your own sobriety. It may not seem like it, but recovery is a life and death issue. The true addict may actually pause and try to debate this one a bit.

You may find yourself wondering, "How can I turn my will and my life over to the care of God, if He doesn't exist (and supposedly neither do I)?" This is how I came to answer those questions for myself. This is how I believe the Shambhala Path of Warriorship, as I know it, can work with the principles that form the basis of the steps of recovery to create a full sober life.

Knowing the meekness of the Tiger, the joy of the Lion, the outrageousness of the Garuda and the wisdom of the Dragon, we can lead a sane, mindful and aware sobriety.

May all beings benefit by this.

Introduction

Someone may tell us that, if we commit ourselves to a particular practice or path, within four weeks we are going to be okay: we are going to be "high" forever. So we try it, and it works - but not forever. After six weeks, at most, or perhaps after only ten days, we begin to come down, and then we begin to panic and wonder what is going on. Usually the most faithful students blame themselves, feeling they mismanaged the practice: "I must have some problem I haven't cleared up yet. I must not have done my confession properly, or given in properly." But that is not the case at all. The problem is the way they were indoctrinated into their spiritual practice. Chogyam Trungpa Rinpoche, *Journey Without Goal*

Whether you have been through the Steps many times, or they are just words on a wall someplace, many people in recovery feel like the quote above. Since they are not "happy, joyous and free" all the time, the program of recovery outlined in the Twelve Steps does not work beyond the abstinence from drinking or drugging. When I began my journey in Shambhala Buddhism I very much felt that way, that somehow I was failing the program or that the program was failing me, because I still felt two steps from the mental ward. The pink cloud was gone and there was no bottle to reach for to bring me the ease and comfort I so desired. What I found was not that the program of recovery was failing me, or I it, but that I needed a few more tools to bolster the spiritual tool kit of the Twelve Step program. I found those tools in the Shambhala teachings and the Shambhala Path of Warriorship. The purpose of this book is to bring awareness of those tools to you.

However before we get into the spiritual tools, I need to give you a little spiritual background on Buddhism and Shambhala.

Shambhala and Recovery

Shambhala is based on the principle that we all want to lead sane and confident lives. As drunks, addicts and users of all types, our lives were everything but sane and confident.

The goal of this book is not to completely lay out the dharma, whether the Buddhadharma or the Shambhala dharma. There are so many wonderful books by scholars and advanced practitioners on those topics that I could not claim to do either any justice. Definitely seek out a practice center. To infuse recovery into our minds and hearts, we need to take it out of the realm of the intellect and place it in the spirit as experience. It has to come out of our heads and into our hearts. We can only do that by practicing, and for that, real people, a real community with one-on-one instruction and group practice, is immeasurably valuable.

Each week we hold a Heart of Recovery meeting at our center. Every Thursday night we open our doors for anyone who is interested in exploring the relationship of addiction and recovery to our personal paths as warriors and meditation practitioners. It is open to all who are interested in the dharma of recovery from addiction and addictive behaviors. Most of all it is open to people of any lineage and any addiction, and those who might be affected by another person's addiction.

As a result each week new people come through the doors. Many of them have never set foot in our center or any center, never meditated, and/or never studied Buddhism. They may be testing the waters of recovery or are in recovery and looking for something different. To explain where they landed, I give an elevator speech that more or less goes like this. This will be our starting point, the Cliff's Notes version, of what Shambhala is and why it could work for others, as it did for me.

Siddhartha

Twenty-five hundred years ago there was a man, a son of a king, Siddhartha Gautama, who one day saw people suffering around him and he wanted to find a way to transcend that cycle of suffering. So he left his wife and child and his life of privilege, and began a variety of extreme religious measures by which he became very adept but no closer to finding his answer. One day he sat down and decided he wasn't going to get up till he figured it out. A life of pleasure was not the answer and a life steeped in pain was not the answer either. Sitting under a bodhi tree day and night, he "awoke" to the truth of suffering, its causes and conditions and more importantly, a way to live without suffering.

Moments before the Siddhartha became enlightened, it is said that Mara,[1] the tempter, came to Siddhartha and threw everything he had at Siddhartha. Mara tried every trick in the book to derail Siddhartha, countless horrors and multitudes of pleasures to keep him from enlightenment. Now Mara holds a special place for me, because Mara is temptation personified. Yet Siddhartha recognized Mara in all his forms and in essence said, "I see you Mara" and with that all the arrows of horrors turned to flowers. Me, I fell for Mara's tricks and lies every time. In time the lies of my addiction created so much pain and suffering that I was brought to my knees. However, not Siddhartha--he saw the lies for what they were. If Siddhartha could see Mara for what he was, then maybe we can too. It is also said that Mara continued to come to see Siddhartha, now known as the Buddha (or awakened one), even after his enlightenment, many more times throughout his life and each time the Buddha treated Mara like an honored guest, a good friend whom he had not seen in a long time. That the Buddha was tempted, that desires and fears still arose within his mind, even after enlightenment brings me solace.

---

[1] In Buddhist cosmology, Mara personifies unwholesome impulses, unskillfulness, the death of the spiritual life. He is a tempter, distracting humans from practicing the spiritual life by making mundane things alluring, or negative seem positive.

That the Buddha knew how to defeat them is a thread of hope for the alcoholic or addict to hold on to.

When Siddhartha arose from under that bodhi tree, he became the awakened one, the Buddha. He began to teach and share what he had discovered. His first teachings became known as the Four Noble Truths, which described that there is suffering, there is a cause of that suffering and therefore a cessation of that suffering and oh, by the way, here is the path out of it.

The Kingdom of Shambhala

At first all who followed the Buddha became monks, leaving their secular lives to learn the dharma, the truth, from the Buddha. This is where the story of Shambhala begins, as there was a king, Dawa Sangpo in Tibetan (Suchandra in Indian), who heard of the Buddha's teachings and wanted to learn from him. Dawa Sangpo went to the Buddha to ask for his teachings. Unfortunately Dawa Sangpo had a dilemma, he could not leave his kingdom, as his people needed him. The Buddha gave a set of teachings that he could follow and not have to leave his kingdom. This allowed Dawa Sangpo to return to his kingdom to create a society based on gentleness and kindness. Thus began the kingdom of Shambhala.

Chogyam Trungpa

In the 20th century, in a corner of Tibet, a 13 month boy was discovered as a reincarnate tulku. In Tibet, a tulku is the reincarnation or return after death, to a physical form of a highly achieved or enlightened Buddhist master. As the 11th Trungpa tulku, Chogyam Trungpa would be raised to become the spiritual and material leader of the Surmang monastery. He was taught two lineages of Buddhism, the Kagyu[2] and the Nyingma[3] lineages. When

---

[2] Kagyu: A Tibetan school of Buddhism tracing its origin back to the Buddha, through the teachings of the Indian yogi Tilopa. Tilopa developed "spontaneous

the Chinese invaded Tibet, Chogyam Trungpa had to make a life or death decision to flee Tibet. So he left Tibet on foot, through the Himalayas into India. After a little time in India he was sent to Oxford, England to learn comparative religions, philosophy and fine arts.

It was there in England and later Scotland that he began to instruct Western students. In 1969 after a solitary retreat in Bhutan, he returned no longer dressed as a monk. His decision to ditch the monastic appearance and lifestyle allowed him to connect to the Western students where they were and as they were. One of the things he saw was that Western students were easily caught in the trap of "spiritual materialism." In other words, they were more concerned with "who is your guru" and collecting practices than the true meanings of the teachings themselves. To teach the dharma Trungpa had to cut through those Western tendencies. Thus he presented Buddhism in a more direct form, a form for the modern Western mind.

This style of teaching and presentation, free from cultural trappings and religious fascination, opened Trungpa up to receive the Shambhala terma. In their simplest form, terma are teachings that have been hidden away, to be discovered at a time and place and by a person who can bring the teachings to light, in a time and place where they are needed. The Shambhala teachings focus on the innate human wisdom and basic goodness at the heart of Buddhism and all religions. Shambhala combines the spiritual path of Buddhism with the idea of a secular enlightenment. It is the continuation of the Buddha's teachings, particularly the Kagyu and Nyingma lineage teachings, in a new manner that is workable by the modern student. These teachings are truly needed in this day of instant

---

insight of realization" through methods taught by the Buddha.

[3] Nyingma: The oldest of the major Tibetan Buddhism schools, often referred to as the school of ancient translations, because it was founded on the early Buddhist scriptures brought to Tibet by Padmasambhava. Focusing on the teaching of Dzogchen, the Great Perfection, as the highest form of realization.

Basic Sobriety

communication, rampant consumerism, environmental upheaval and physical, emotional and spiritual degradation.

Walking into a Shambhala meditation hall does not feel like a traditional Buddhist shrine room. All the traditional teachings are there, but presented in a unique way, combining the insight, devotion and practice of the original teachings with the grounded sense of the Tibetan culture from which Trungpa came, along with a more universal sense of engaging society. Thus the teachings of basic goodness, windhorse[4], drala[5] and Ashe[6] feel like a sword cutting through everything we thought we were getting ourselves into when we thought, *let's study Buddhism.* They are presented in a language that seems to agree with everything we have felt in our souls.

So how might the Shambhala teachings help?

First, you do not have to be a Buddhist or give up our old "higher power" to get on the Shambhala path. Even if you do not decide to follow the Buddhist path, the Way of Shambhala can be a complete path in and of itself. It will help you develop and establish a daily meditation practice that is steady enough and grounded

---

[4] Windhorse: Will be described in greater detail further on, but it is a "self existing energy" we all have within us. "The *'wind'* principle of basic goodness is strong and exuberant and brilliant. It can actually radiate tremendous power in your life. But at the same time, basic goodness can be ridden, which is the principle of the *'horse'*. By following the disciplines of warriorship, particularly the discipline of letting go, you can harness the wind of goodness." p. 84, *Shambhala: Sacred Path of the Warrior*

[5] Drala: (Tibetan: "dra", enemy or opponent; "la", above): "beyond the enemy". "Unconditioned wisdom and power of the world that are beyond any dualism, therefore Drala is above any enemy or conflict. It is wisdom beyond aggression. p. 103, *Shambhala: Sacred Path of the Warrior*

[6] Ashe: "Tibetan: primordial or first stroke. In the Shambhala teachings A-, primordial or first, is the open space of mind before the first thought, or first gesture; that first thought or gesture is -she. Ashe is the power to express basic goodness and is also known as "the essence of life." Ashe symbolizes primordial confidence and compassion." from Jeremy Hayward's *Warrior - King of Shambhala - Remembering Chogyam Trungpa*

enough to help you face your fears and aid your recovery. You do not have to be a Shambhalian or even a Buddhist if you do not want to, for these teachings to be beneficial.

The teachings begin with who you are when you walk through the door. You start with all the tragedy and pain, all the childhood traumas and adult dramas. We get to bring it all to the path. All the muck is welcomed. The way of Shambhala is a non-theistic path, which combines the historic teachings of the Buddha and Tibetan Buddhism with everyday modern life. It also grabs pinches and dashes from other lineages and enlightened societies throughout history. The Shambhala path is grounded in a basic human wisdom that is relevant to all.

One of the fundamental concepts, the ground from which it all springs is: basic goodness. These two words are trying to describe something ultimately indescribable. Trungpa went beyond the idea of Buddha nature, because even the phrase "Buddha nature" has many cultural and spiritual preconceptions. It is from basic goodness that the Buddha arose; it is a deep, primordial sense of the unconditioned. It is beyond or before even the ideas of good and bad. It is good because it is our natural state.

Wait a second--you are telling me I am good? Not bad? Not evil? Not broken? Have you seen my life?

How might this change the game? What changes inside my mind and heart if I am basically good instead of inherently a flawed person? Recently a teacher handed out a list which had two columns, one for words for "basic" and one for words for "goodness". The point of this list was to illustrate that we should not get fixed even on the word pair of basic goodness. Still, basic goodness is the phrase that you will hear most often and the phrase that starts to be the sand in the ointment of my self-hating, self-deprecating, and self-destructive view of myself.

Walking into a Shambhala shrine room, above the shrine is a thangka. A thangka is a painting on linen depicting spiritual beings and teachings. You may notice something different about the picture if you look a little more closely. It is not the Buddha in the picture.

Basic Sobriety

Who is it? Seated on a celestial throne is a (male/female) Rigden and if you look closely, above the Rigden and supported by the throne of the Rigden like a jewel on the top of a spire sits the Buddha. The Buddha was the earthly manifestation of enlightened leadership. The Rigden combines the sacred and secular aspects of Shambhala. One definition of Rigden is "family holder". These primordial beings have never known hope or fear. They represent the basic enlightened nature of all beings. They are the embodiment of enlightened essence, which is our nature as well.

So not only is the Rigden royal and enlightened, he still engages the world as a family holder. This is one of the fundamental principles of the Shambhala teachings to engage the world, to be family holders ourselves. Family is a grounding concept; it provides us an earthly base of living. We are all part of some sort of family, whether we like it or not. Family was there at beginning of life and where most of our negative habits (i.e., buttons) were installed.

In the same manner that Twelve Step meetings help us live for the remaining 23 hours a day, so too do the Shambhala teachings endeavor to teach us how to live on and off the meditation cushion. This is not a go off into the woods type of practice. The analogy is to engage the world at the kitchen sink level, to utilize the teachings in our ordinary lives. We have the ability to uncover the inherent beauty in that ordinariness to the point of life being extraordinary.

Every part of our life is workable and every aspect of our life is to be used as part of the path. No part of life is excluded; in fact, there is no time off for good behavior. Life is there to tickle us and break our hearts. The Rigden is there to remind all of us that we can be the rulers of our world, just not in the self-centered, all for me and none for you manner we attempted before we put down our addictions. The Rigden symbolizes the possibility of becoming a good person, a good family member, a good parent and spouse (or step-parent and ex-spouse if you are those as well).

Right when you walk in the door, you are welcomed into the Shambhala family. You've always been part of the family, you just didn't know it yet.

Milarepa and Protectors

It wasn't long after I walked through the doors of the St. Petersburg Shambhala center that I learned that goodness can be realized in this lifetime, that the highest levels of enlightened realization can occur in this, not immeasurable lifetimes. One of the best examples of enlightenment in one lifetime is Milarepa (born 1052 and died 1135 CE). Milarepa is the wonderful true story of a boy whose early life begins wealthy and turns to a life of hardship and resentment after his father dies. As a teenager, pushed by his mother, he learns black magic, which he uses to kill a number of people who had wronged him and his family. Realizing the nature of what he did, Milarepa goes off to find the dharma as a way to cleanse his karmic actions. He goes all in (like all good alcoholics and addicts have a tendency to do) and, after a number of years, he realizes the nature of himself and everything, i.e., enlightenment.

So not only are the practices of Shambhala Buddhism realizable in one lifetime, they could also be realized by a murderer / sinner such as Milarepa.

In the back corner of the shrine room, there is a scary-looking fellow with many eyes and arms. He is not an evil demon but a protector. The story goes that around 760 CE Padmasambhava, also known as Guru Rinpoche, was invited to Tibet. All the demons came out to fight trying to protect their land and to protect their own ego trips. Padmasambhava tamed them all, putting into practice the tantric philosophy that no energy (or person or spirit) is inherently bad or evil, and so this demon-looking thing became a protector of the dharma. His name is Mahakala and he is a wisdom protector. For the alcoholic / addict it reminds us how our greatest demons, faults and tragedies will become not only our greatest teachers, but the way to help others. Our demons become our protectors.

The horrors of my own drinking are what keep me safest. Now I can use all of that to open my heart and help others. I am that Mahakala.

I am that Mahakala just as I am that Rigden.

So are you.

The Path of the Dignities

In the typical Shambhala meditation hall hang four banners. On each one of these banners is one of four dignities: the Tiger, Snow Lion, Garuda (a legendary Tibetan bird, born full grown from its egg and never touches the earth) and Dragon. These dignities symbols of a path and process of training to help us to know ourselves and to engage in the world. It is a path to developing authentic presence. Much like the Twelve Steps, they can be seen as both independent entities while always remaining interdependent.

If you could imagine your legs as the Tiger, your torso as the Snow Lion, your chest and shoulders as the Garuda and your head as the Dragon, you would metaphorically have a complete person. We would be a complete person, a "whole" person, a Warrior of Shambhala. The qualities come together as the grounded, humble meekness of the Tiger, the vibrant and joyful Snow Lion, the visionary perspective of the outrageous Garuda and the inscrutable wisdom of the Dragon all come together to develop a complete person, a complete warrior in the world. The qualities of these dignities are like guideposts along the path of our journey. We may never fully achieve these qualities, much like we may never be fully done with the Steps. The qualities help maintain the direction we head; they lead us along the path, ever reminding us that it is "progress not perfection".

Being a Warrior of Shambhala does not mean we are to become someone who is aggressive and destructive, in the assumed sense of the word, but someone who is brave, living a life of fearlessness, gentleness and intelligence. A warrior is not afraid to face himself and to do battle with all that separates him (or her) from the world. As a Warrior of Shambhala our purpose is to engage the world and society, through our work, family and actions. The warrior leads a complete and full life, right in the midst of all of life's challenges.

Turning Poison into Medicine

In all the research I did about Shambhala, when we first started attending open houses. Two things stood out and since they will inevitably come up for you, let's bring them out right now, much like he did. First was that Chogyam Trungpa was a brilliant teacher and meditation instructor and a pivotal voice in bringing Buddhism to America. He accomplished much in his short time here in America. Second, there are some crazy stories about drinking, drugs and women. These stories are not just about the sangha members in the age of sex, drugs and rock and roll, but about the man himself. His death was most likely a typical alcoholic death, cirrhosis of the liver.[7] And this is to be my guru?

Each of us will have to come to our own understanding of the root teacher, his teachings, his methods, his activities and how that all impacts the lineage today. Since I was not there for any of it firsthand, I cannot tell you if any of the stories are true or not. Yet, from my interactions with his students I believe that lots of them are true. The legend of Chogyam Trungpa is filled with amazingly wonderful, magical stories and amazingly questionable stories. Driving my daughter to school this morning, I was reminded of the story of how his driver was speeding along well over the speed limit, with Trungpa asleep in the back, suddenly Trungpa shot up in his seat and started chanting in Tibetan as they sped past a cop in speed trap who didn't blink an eye. Amazed, his driver turned around and

---

[7]Mitchell Levy on Chronicles Radio Presents. November 1, 2008.

Basic Sobriety

asked what that was all about, to which Trungpa replied, "I just felt we needed a gap right there." Of course there are the less than magical stories about parties and drugs and sex. A common explanation I received is that it was the 70s and it was a different time. Trungpa hid nothing so there were no skeletons. But is that explanation enough?

That Trungpa may have died an alcoholic death tells me that the disease of alcoholism respects no one. No matter how great you are, no matter how many lifetimes you've lived, no matter how realized you are, alcohol doesn't give a shit. It's pretty impersonal like that. For most people, alcohol is neither for nor against them-- same with food, sex or drugs. They can take them or leave them. For those of us who are so smitten, whatever its origin or vehicle, it will plunge us into the hungry ghost realm for what seems an eternity. The Vajrayana, or Esoteric Buddhist teaching about alcohol is that it can be used as an elixir; much the same way Padmasambhava turned the demons into protectors, alcohol can be turned from something dangerous into something beneficial. However, even with all that realization, Trungpa was still a man, an ordinary man, an extraordinary man, but nonetheless a real human being.

"Alcoholic is just a label and you must shed the use of such defining labels," a teacher has said to me on more than one occasion. True, most of the labels we attach to ourselves come and go as easily as changing clothes. Some labels I held on to well past their usefulness. Most of them have changed over the decades. The labels I put on my drinking changed over the years as well.

Drinking started out cute and fun in high school, with the worst damage being broken friendships, bad hangovers and lost jobs. That changed to be a little bit more "costly" in college, with three alcohol-induced trips to the emergency room my senior year. I needed to recuperate after that "strenuous" senior year by working a low level job and drinking every night until I got sick and tired of that life and tried to get a real job and step out on my own. Then drinking was something that had to be controlled but frequently got out of hand. When drinking changed from desire to need, I cannot tell you. Even going off to college, to a major party university far from home, I packed three bottles of liquor, figuring that would hold me over long enough to figure out where to get more, indicating that the subtle fear of a life without alcohol was already beginning to grow inside me well before I was of legal drinking age. The disease of alcoholism is a progressive disease and so one day, it began to take on a whole new sense of urgency. Drinking changed from something I thought I just needed to make the day or night more enjoyable, to my being completely terrified of being sober for a day. With that those four horsemen appeared and it took on proportions only few know. If you are reading this book, maybe they have visited you as well.

In the rooms you hear about people going back out because they systematically forgot all that recovery taught them, and no matter how they changed the label or covered it up, the disease was still there. If we drink again, even after decades without drinking, we are right back where we left off in a short span of time. *Therefore in my opinion "alcoholic" is not a label. It is a rule for this body, in this lifetime. As surely as I cannot drink arsenic, I cannot drink alcohol, or partake of any other mood-altering substance or behavior. Period.*

Now, if Trungpa was a drunk, what does it mean about his teachings and his legacy? In my opinion the answer to that question has nothing to with him and everything to do with me. What is the result of adding the word "alcoholic" to the list of labels we use for Trungpa? Or more personally for ourselves? Immediately all of society's shameful taboos about the word come into play. Alcoholic has a great many negative connotations and misconceptions. If I can negate all of his accomplishments and teachings with that one word, then can I subsequently negate all my accomplishments as well? Not one thing in my life will be of value because of the connotations associated with the word "alcoholic". If I believe what society tells me about the disease of addiction, then an alcoholic can accomplish nothing of value.

Can I really believe that? That nothing I will ever do will mean anything? Nothing I did in the past, nothing I will do in the future will mean a thing because, "well, he was an alcoholic." No, I cannot believe that everything I do going forward will be worthless. Each day I don't drink, I have a chance at doing something worthwhile and good. Even if the only good I do that day is giving my daughter a hug, smiling at my wife or not making things worse by picking up a drink. The laws of karma themselves teach me that what I do in this moment has immense value, as the positive seeds I plant today will sprout somewhere down the line. But more on karma later.

5th Precept[8] - Do Not Take Intoxicants

I do not agree that you can transform the poison of alcohol into an elixir. Maybe some can, maybe some really realized beings can, but I cannot. Thich Nhat Hanh describes how if we are drinking whiskey mindfully we will feel how the effects take us away from our ability to be mindful and therefore we will stop. HA! Just trying to eat a chocolate chip cookie mindfully I see the problem with my addict mind. My mind will always want more and more and more! "Therefore, the main problem of the alcoholic centers in his mind, rather than his body." (Big Book of AA, p. 23) Mindfully eating a chocolate chip cookie, I can follow the rise and fall of the taste sensation. Paying such close attention to that peak and the saddening fall makes me immediately reach for another cookie, and another, and another.

There is a really good reason why there is the 5th precept against intoxicants. There is a parable about a monk who is approached by a beautiful woman with a goat and a jug of wine. She

---

[8] Basic training rules (more or less) observed by all practicing lay Buddhists. They are 1) Refrain from killing, 2) Refrain from taking that which is not given, 3) Refrain from lying, 4) Refrain from sexual misconduct and 5) Refrain from taking intoxicants. These will be discussed in detail in Step Four.

asks the monk what he would rather do: kill the goat, have sex with her or drink the wine. Thinking that drinking the wine would have the least karmic impact, he drank the wine. In the morning, he woke to find he drank all the wine, killed the goat and had sex with the woman. When I was drunk there was a good chance I too would break the other 4 precepts and once I started drinking, I was getting drunk.

I cannot take Trungpa's inventory, nor anyone else's. Truth is truth. Dharma is dharma. As the Buddha said so many years ago (and I'm paraphrasing), "This is what I did; see if it works for you as well." We need to put the teachings to the test and not just believe them blindly. We also need to have the wisdom to know what to accept and what to reject. To reject the teachings because the teacher was possibly a drunk means I need to reject myself as well because I too was a drunk. It is only by looking at both sides of the picture that a logical answer arises. One does not overrule the other and one does not negate the other. How I view myself relates to how I view the teachings and how I view the teachings relates to how I view myself. The proof ultimately needs to be discovered for yourself.

Even though it has been around thirty years since Trungpa's death, his drinking and his other behaviors remain a divided and polemic topic. While most alcoholics seem to systematically tear down the world and people around them, Trungpa accomplished amazing things in a short period of time here in America, the least of which was starting the largest group of Buddhist meditation centers in the West and beginning a worldwide community that still thrives today. It is said, and I believe, that Trungpa gave himself tirelessly to students. The stories of the great Kagyu leaders, the reincarnates of his holiness the Karmapa, tell of how they typically died early because they took on so much negative karma and energy of those around them. One of the most interesting tidbits of stories that I have heard is, not that as the Big Book describes, that "He is always more or less insanely drunk" (Big Book of AA, p. 21) but rather that Trungpa would go from drunk to insanely sober in a snap.

Basic Sobriety

While his death may have been as a result of his drinking,[9] he was recognized by many of the great Tibetan masters of the day as a mahasiddha. A mahasiddha is one who is connected with the highest levels of spiritual enlightenment while choosing to help others. The Kagyu and Nyingma lineage is full of such great teachers. Trungpa was also part of a great line of enlightened crazy wisdom teachers, in that they would do anything that was necessary to help their students to achieve enlightenment and if that meant at just the right time a slap in the face with a sandal was needed, then so be it.

The bodies and minds we have in this lifetime cannot process alcohol, drugs, sex or food like other people do. Our addictions do not negate our basic goodness, or our ability to achieve spiritual fulfillment. Drinking alcohol is just not an option for this body and this lifetime; it is a rule for this body. Maybe you have a body and mind like mine?

I believe the Shambhala teachings can help us to improve our recovery, to help achieve that seemingly impossible recovery "from a hopeless state of mind and body" (Big Book of AA, Foreword to the First Edition). The following chapters will, show you ways in which that is possible. They are the ways that I have seen and experienced the steps and the teachings. If you have an issue or a question, by all means doubt it, sit with it, and discuss it with fellow members and teachers. In the end only you will know what to accept and what to reject. Most things I initially rejected were not based on the merits or validity of the teachings. I rejected them because they threatened the beliefs I was comfortable with. They turned out to be the truth, and believing the truth is the easier, softer way. I once chose to believe in a world that did not exist and I discovered it could only result in one thing—suffering.

---

[9] In a November 2008 interview, when asked, "What was he ill with? What did he die of?" Trungpa's doctor, Dr. Mitchell Levy, replied, "He had chronic liver disease related to his alcoholic intake over many years."

Step One

We admitted we were powerless over alcohol - that our lives had become unmanageable. (Big Book of AA)

I did not drink like the average person. Of course I did not drink to be average, but to fit in and be someone other than who I was. Early in my teens, I worked for a local grocery store with an antiquated beer cooler, with no security camera. What started as taking beer for after work became taking beer for our lunch breaks, which became drinking as soon as possible in the day. I worked very hard that summer, punching in at 6 a.m. and working almost every day. Therefore, I got drunk every day. That taught me a few very important lessons about drinking and living: how to hide the fact that I was drunk while still appearing functional and that there were certain beers that caused me to get sick. Oh no, it was not the amount of them I drank, it was those particular brands of beer--those were the ones to be avoided.

Twenty-plus years later, I found myself sitting in a dark corner of a church parking lot. I could not go home. If I went home I did not know how to not get drunk. I was past all the tricks I could come up with to control my drinking. If I could just go home and only have 10 beers, just enough to get me to sleep, I would have been happy. That experiment had ended in failure many times before. I had long been past the days of drinking in bars, of drinking socially, of drinking with other people around. For the last few years it was just me every night on the back porch, a case of beer, a pack of cigarettes, and a bottle of Jack on the counter. When I was drinking I went nowhere and I saw no one. This was drinking to keep the terror away. This was drinking because I had to drink. Sober you had to face the world. Sober you are naked and raw, without any shield or armor. Sober you have to feel. It had been a long time since I could face the day or the night without getting drunk. This is the terror of loneliness that few people know. That was what awaited me if I went back home that night.

There were no more friends to call, no more family members to bail me out of trouble yet again. No more women to say "poor baby". The gutter was calling my name and I could not take that last step. There I sat, crying my eyes out in the car. I sat there trying to figure out where to go. Would there be a sign? Maybe there would be someone waving people in? Had I not been absolutely terrified of another night of drinking I would have turned around and gone home. I was desperate, which is exactly where one needs to be in order to be open to a program of recovery.

An Honest Look

There is a small window between the moment of desperation and the moment of forgetting how bad it really was. The problem is that since you are your own filter, you have no clue how bad it really was and soon enough you convince yourself that regardless of all the evidence to the contrary, it wasn't that bad.

Let me tell you, it was much worse than you ever realized. Our egos have been beaten to the point of submission. The goal of the Twelve Steps of recovery is to create a fundamental shift away from selfish and self-centered living. The Sakyong, the spiritual leader of the Shambhala Buddhist lineage, calls this selfish and self-centered living the "me plan". The fruition is for us to live free of the "me plan" (Ruling Your World by Sakyong Mipham).

They say that this is the only step we have to do 100 percent. We need to honestly know that we are an alcoholic and that we cannot drink (or drug or whatever our addiction) like other people. Without this honesty we will only scratch the surface. We will not fully embrace our addiction. We will keep our addiction at arm's length. It is only when we begin to open the door of honesty that we will begin to see what we really were doing to ourselves and others through our addiction. It is only with honesty that we will be able to get value of the remaining steps and path.

Just becoming honest about my drinking was a big step. I had lied to doctors, therapists, employers, lovers, and family about the amount I drank and how often. I hid my drinking and blamed everyone else as the cause of my drinking. Getting honest about the simple fact that I could not stop once I started and I could not stay stopped when I wanted to stay stopped was a huge step. In high school I joked to my friends about how many of the "20 questions to determine if you are an alcoholic" I answered yes to. Over the years I would typically make statements like, "Sure there were times in the past where drinking got away from me, but I'm OK now." Bull. Didn't everyone drink a case a beer every night because of their crappy boss, job, wife, day, or whatever you wanted to fill in the blank with? If it was sunny I drank. If it rained I drank. I no longer needed any sorts of excuses, I just needed to drink. Deeper levels of honesty would come later, with each step, but for now the door was opened here. I needed to be open about my drinking because I just couldn't keep the lie going one day longer. Even if we are ignorant of all our other problems, just admitting and conceding that we are addicted to one thing is a momentous step.

Without honesty being an alcoholic or addict is just theoretical. It remains just in the head. We need to get it into our heart. I need to honestly believe, in my heart, that I am an alcoholic. Whatever your addiction, it is there in our hearts that we must know it as true. When it stays in my head, I can convince myself otherwise. I can come up with all sorts of reasons and theories, case studies and case law to prove myself innocent. I must honestly believe in my heart that I am an alcoholic, not that you believe I am an alcoholic. Nor can I do this so the wife or judge or partner or job will let us back in. When I do it for others it is theoretical, another game of manipulation and control. Being honest meant seeing what I was doing for what it really was. We need to see our drinking, or drug use, or whatever our addiction is for what it truly was. This initial state of honesty, this honesty about not being able to continue the life we had been leading, must be done before we can start the rest of the steps.

Powerless and Unmanageable

Step One contains two concepts that we need to see to fully understand the beginning of the path to recovery: "powerless" and "unmanageable". On the surface level, we must concede that we are powerless over our addiction or substance or behavior of choice. In the beginning we may have had some control, our use may have been "recreational", but we were long past those days of recreational use. For everyone, this powerlessness is slightly different. For some it could mean that we say, "Tonight I am only having 2 beers and going home," but have 20. For others, it could mean that one out of four nights we drink, it becomes a blackout train wreck, but we can never tell which night of the four it will be. Each night we take the chance and roll the dice. One night we go out, have 2 beers and go home, but the next one under the same conditions we wake up the next morning not knowing where we are, what happened or where the car is. For each of us it is different; we are spree, binge, daily, social, solo, fill-in-the-blank kind of drinkers, but what we all share, in one form or another, is that once we start all bets are off as to what the results will be. That makes life pretty unmanageable in and of itself but sadly, that is usually not enough for most of us.

Unmanageable, as a friend says, is "things getting worse faster than we can lower our standards". Whether our standards are all the way to the ground or they are just starting to fall is only a matter of time and how deep into our 'ism' we are. No matter how far down we have gone, we have been trying to hold it all together and it just won't stay still. Maybe to the outward world we have it all together, but inwardly it is all a terrible mess. All the insanity of our life falling apart around us generally turns us back to our addiction, which in turn causes the problems to worsen, continuing a wonderfully horrendous downward spiral. Each of us will have different levels of unmanageability and what will be enough for some will be bearable to others. They say that AA started out just for the low-bottom drunk, but eventually the "bottom" was raised so each of us could set our own bottom. For some that first DUI or rehab will be enough, for others it will take a bit more and some will have no DUIs and happy homes still intact.

You do not need to ride the elevator all the way to the bottom. You can get off at any time. The Big Book of AA talks about the "potential alcoholic". Maybe you are saying to yourself, *Sure I have these similarities to what you are saying, but I still have not gone all the way over the line.* In fact many of us danced on that line for some time. Many of us have erased and redrawn new lines numerous times. If you are wondering if you have a problem or may even be a potential alcoholic, it is suggested to try a period of abstinence or a period of controlled drinking. Even the potential alcoholic will have a hard time staying sober for any serious length of time. Many of us will get drunk on the first day of a new month; having proven we are not alcoholic by staying dry for a period of time, we celebrate by getting drunk. Getting drunk to celebrate proving we are not drunks is truly wonderful logic and could be proof that we have a problem. Sadly, most of us will not see the writing on the wall until it is too late.

Addiction is a progressive disease; "it only gets worse, never better." Some may be able to pull it back together, given sufficient cause or reason. Others will need more research to determine their status, and many will not want to hear what others are saying until it is too late. You may have tried various methods to control your addiction, possibly with some success at first but then failure. None method has quite worked and your addiction will eventually win out every time.

You can always drink tomorrow, right? So for today let us just put it off till tomorrow. It is this kind of thinking we can utilize in early sobriety (or anytime) to postpone picking up, sometimes just taking it hour by hour or minute by minute. In that gap, that space, we have a chance to do something that may give us enough peace to allow us to hold out a little longer. Even if you are just a potential alcoholic or addict, just not picking up today, the steps and the Shambhala path of Warriorship could be extremely beneficial.

Three Characteristics We All Share

To say that life is unmanageable would seem to imply that there is a manageable life somewhere out there in the first place. Powerless would also seem to imply that somewhere we have power. There once was a list as long as my arm of things that I thought I could control, and on more deluded days that list grew exponentially. Isn't it true that the atom is influenced by the mind? Or so I believed. Thus all sorts of power of positive thinking and mental coincidences were completely blown out of proportion. The belief that somehow I could manage life would mean that numerous laws of the universe did not work. I believed that I could somehow lasso that out-of-control bastard of a universe and get it to do what I wanted it to do. Society likes to foster that idea upon us and so I thought if I could just do X, Y and Z better everything would fall into place. However life, by default or definition, is unmanageable.

Life is a never-ending, constant stream of impermanence,[10] suffering[11] and emptiness.[12] These are the three characteristics, marks of existence, shared by all people and beings according to the Buddhist teachings. However, these issues are what are misconceived to mean that there is no purpose, no meaning, and no reason for life. The Big Book refers to this belief as "it would follow

---

[10] Impermanence (Annica in pali) teaches that all conditioned things are in a state of flux and change, that nothing will remain forever as it is.

[11] Suffering (Dukkha in pali) or dissatisfaction, since nothing is permanent, then nothing in the physical world can bring us lasting satisfaction. This is the First Noble Truth of Buddhism.

[12] Emptiness or no-self (Anatta in pali) in that our perception of self does not exist as a single entity or essence. That we, and all things, are made up of conditions, experiences, and pieces, but nowhere is there a single self existing entity that we can say is 'Me'.

that life originated out of nothing, means nothing, and proceeds nowhere." For now, I ask that we remain open and aware that these misconceptions about impermanence, suffering and emptiness do not mean that life is without value or meaning. Impermanence does not mean we should take an F-it attitude of "everyone dies one day anyway." Suffering does not mean that we have no say in our life unfolding such that it will only bring us misery. Emptiness does not mean that I am nothing, that I do not exist. When we look at these three characteristics of life, when we unlock some of their magic, what we see is that life is absolutely incredible and should be cherished. That we are, right now, amazing, brilliant beings. Whatever you are doing, whatever is going on around you and wherever you are right now is an incredible moment, which will never exist for anyone else ever again. So enjoy the magic. Yet when we were drinking and using, life felt a lot more like it was without magic than full of magic. Life definitely was anything but amazing, to me, at the end of my drinking.

Control

All I really wanted was for each day to remain relatively the same, then I could figure out how to manage it. If I could manage it, then I had control. Asked today what I have power over, the list is extremely short. From the moment I start my day, I am relying on things that are completely outside my control, beginning with the alarm clock beside my bed, made by others and running on electricity which comes from who knows where. Then begins the barrage of possibilities: where did the cat throw up last night, what are the kids doing, what is my wife doing, what is the weather like? And that is all before getting my feet to the floor. Navigating that morning chaos, I make it out the door to find the next test is the drive to work, which most of us just love, with of all those people and conditions that we cannot control. I work for a large corporation, so there are clients and bosses and stockholders, and what is the economy in China doing today? Maybe you've tried to manage and control all these aspects of your life as well? We all have a wide array of means and methods by which we tried to control and manipulate people, places and things around us so that we can have a "good" day. It can be pretty exhausting trying to control all those things which are completely out of our control.

Bringing it in tighter, to myself, can I even control myself? Of course I can, right? How much goes on in our bodies that we cannot control? I am no scientist but how much of eating a meal is automatic, regardless of how mindful or present I might be. I bite, I chew and my body takes care of the rest. How many times does my body not do what I want it to do, things like sweating or burping or farting? I physically cannot hit a golf ball the way my mind envisions. The list goes on, but what we see is that most of what I think I control, even within myself, is a myth. Try for a moment and stand up. You have a thought or intention to "stand up" and somehow all the muscles and tendons in your body make it so. You really didn't have much input beyond the initial command to "stand up"--maybe a little course correction here and there, but most of it is automatic. Then of course there are the thoughts themselves; ten minutes on the meditation cushion shows me how my thoughts are all over the place. They seemingly arise from nothing and if I can let them go, go back to nothing. Even when we are trying to remain focused on the task at hand, our mind is uncontrolled. How my mind interprets the signals it receives from the world is usually in doubt as well, tinted and painted by my emotions and memories.

At first we prove to ourselves that we are powerless over our addiction or substance of choice. Then we see that our powerlessness extends to almost everything. Lastly we see that the carefully constructed and defended entity that I once thought almost godlike is really mostly out of my control. Talk about a humbling realization. Powerlessness is a realization that only can be seen after hitting rock bottom. Rock bottom shatters the big illusions.

Suffering

What the Buddha taught, in a nutshell, was the reality that no matter what, we will suffer in this life through our own passions, aggressions or ignorance. All of this powerlessness and unmanageability creates suffering. We remain ignorant of the three marks of existence: that things are impermanent and will change, that all our passions, aggressions and ignorance will continue to not bring us happiness, and that the way we view the world and ourselves is incorrect. What is wonderful is that these fallacies are great places to begin once we see the truth of them. Our addictions opened that door wide. The way that we had been living our lives was not working.

Each and every one of us have spent our entire lives trying to find our own path out of suffering. However, what started out as a natural and sane instinct "to avoid suffering" would later become a repetitive habit of avoidance which inevitably resulted in creating more and more suffering--exactly the opposite of what we intended. For a period of time, beer and liquor seemed to free me of suffering; life seemed livable. I could dance and sing and talk to women, and life seemed enjoyable--until it wasn't.

In fact our suffering is much more pervasive and subtle than we realized. Since suffering exists it has to have come from somewhere; it has to have a beginning. We are the ones who create and continue to create our own suffering, through our grasping, ignorance or passion. This grasping, ignorance and passion create a continual cycle of suffering (what the Buddha called samsara). As long as we keep chasing those three items--passion, aggression and ignorance--we keep ending up right where we began, in samsara, the cycle of death and rebirth. The way out of that is to be free of the cycle of suffering. Since suffering exists there must be the absence of suffering. There is no dark without light, no hot without cold, no this without that. Therefore we could not even realize we were suffering if the absence of suffering was not possible. Since we create our own suffering, we could conceivably end our own suffering.

The way each of us experiences suffering will vary from moment to moment throughout our lifetime. Our shrine room at the center in St. Petersburg, Florida is a wonderful example of this moment-to-moment suffering. It is too warm, too cold, the air is about to turn on or when will it go off? You are constantly in a state of wanting the room to be just slightly different than it is and in that rare moment it is just right, the air kicks on and off we go again. Yet to say we suffer is a very vague and nebulous concept. It could be said that suffering is caused by that sense of discomfort I illustrated above, but Trungpa describes it more specifically as a sense of anxiety. Suffering is caused by a basic anxiety that is happening all the time. This seems to be particularly acute in alcoholics and addicts, as you often hear phrases like "I never felt comfortable in my own skin" when people tell their stories. As a result of this anxiety we do all sorts of things to try to make ourselves feel comfortable. We try various methods of aggression (pushing away), methods of passion (pulling in), and methods of ignorance (not caring). These methods may work for a moment but they are not lasting and as a result we find ourselves still there with that anxiety. Many times we find ourselves feeling worse off than before. These ongoing habits create the vicious cycle of samsara, a cycle of suffering that we have possibly perpetuated for thousands of lifetimes. Each of us is constantly struggling to ease our own suffering, in the process making ourselves and others feel bad. Worse, those others are doing it too! Even those so-called "normies" are also perpetuating their own anxiety, their own struggle, and creating their own samsara. Then their anxiety and our anxiety work off each other, generating new and further anxiety. It is one big mess out there, and we were trying to exert some "power" and "manage" this.

While all people suffer, we as alcoholics and addicts seemed to take it up a notch. "Woe is me!" was our great cry. No one seemed to suffer like we did, and since we are the center of our universe, no one could possibly suffer as we did. As a friend likes to say, "My broken pinkie is much worse that your broken leg". Admitting we are suffering is Step One, both on the Buddhist path and the recovery path. Admitting both defeats will be the path to victory.

Bravery of the Warrior

To suffer must mean that there is the possibility of freedom from suffering. In the Shambhala tradition freedom from powerlessness and suffering in all its forms is accomplished by developing authentic presence and realizing our basic goodness. The path to developing authentic presence is the path of the Four Dignities of the Warrior. The path is a journey which begins by showing us how we are trapped by our own egos and habits and leads us to experience the wisdom and freedom of a mind free from fixation. The beginning of this path of the warrior is the Warrior of Meek, which is symbolized by the Tiger.

Just as before, it seems like contradiction laid upon contradiction. I am reduced to powerlessness and suffering and yet you are telling me the answer lies within the Path of the Warrior? Warrior? Give up the fight and pick up a white, you may ask? How can warriorship deal with the consummate failure of my individual battle against my addiction and my seeming failure of a life? And how is this Tiger warrior Meek?

The type of warrior that we are discussing is not the "all blood and guts and glory" kind that we have been habitually trained in Western society to emulate, whether in the classroom or office or on the sports field. Warriorship starts with our own personal bravery. The first act of bravery is the decision to get clean and sober or to no longer partake in our addiction or addictive behaviors, even if it is just for one day. This is a momentous and terrifying moment that most of us will only reach when we experience the pain of rock bottom, because the thought of living without our addiction is as scary as living without air. You do not have to hit "rock bottom" to experience this bravery; you can do so at any time. This bravery is open to anyone, regardless of whether you are an addict or not. As we have seen, all people suffer and all people have habits--neurotic habits and pleasant habits--but habits just the same.

Here bravery is the bravery to take our seat on the cushion, to try to be with ourselves exactly as we are. Most of us have avoided this moment for quite some time. Just as it takes bravery to take our seat in the rooms of recovery, it takes incredible bravery to sit and meditate. The path of warriorship is not about going on some blissed-out spiritual trip. In this case meditation means sitting with ourselves and whatever may arise, including our feelings. We are asking ourselves to hold our seat and not run away from the cushion when desires, pain, or regret arise. These desires may be subtle: they may simply be the desire to lie down and watch TV or finish an email. It may be the desire of our addiction. When we are sitting, we are willing to be with ourselves, to simply be--to be who we are, as we are. We have used and abused in an effort to avoid being with ourselves. Anything but that, anything but having to be me. This is why it takes an immense amount of bravery to sit down without entertainment or avoidance. Every time we sit down to meditate, we should remind ourselves of the importance and power of that bravery.

Bravery and Basic Goodness

Sitting with ourselves is the beginning of learning bravery, of learning to be with ourselves and the world without deception. This is the same bravery as learning to be in the world clean and sober. It is this bravery that begins the path of the Warrior. Here we are calling on the qualities of the warrior, of someone who is not afraid of who they are or the world around them. In those first few shaky days and weeks of sobriety, this idea of someone who is unafraid may seem impossible, so we simply set our aim in that direction. This will be a journey of "progress not perfection" (Big Book of AA). Ultimately, a warrior is not defined by his armor or his weapons, but by his lack of armor, his exposure to the world with an open and tender hear, the tender heart of sadness. This tender heart is opened fearlessly so that it may embrace all things. The sadness is not the depression type of sadness we felt in our addiction, but from experiencing a joyful open heart. We are so tender and alive that we wish we could share this feeling with everyone. But it's not as simple as passing the joint to the next person, and we know it. We can't just make them feel as joyful as we feel, thus we have a sense of sadness. It is quite a journey and it would be incredible to just throw off our armor and rush out into the world, but most of us will make this journey slowly. Little by little, we need to knock the rust off our armor before we can even begin to think of taking it off.

To expose your true nature takes great bravery, dignity and discipline. This is warriorship, to be present with our own mind. The first thing we learn when we sit down to meditate is to let go of our thoughts--to let them come and go. We are not trying to stop the thoughts. We do not have to fight them at all. When we can do that, we become "all victorious" because we did not even have to battle; we have won before we even needed to step into the ring. That is the fruition, if we can get there, but every tree must start as a seed. We are planting that seed now.

Each step along the way is a step to becoming a warrior without armor. It will be a great journey of self discovery. We have hidden ourselves away deep inside, pretending to be someone or something we are not. We may feel that our own true person is completely lost, that because of our addictions we are no longer worth anything, rotten to the core. Many of us did and experienced things that would make a priest blush. We are full of fears and that is a wonderful place to be, because it is through fear that we will discover fearlessness down the road. Each time we can sit and open our heart just a little more allows us to ease into all of the things that frightened us. When we sit, returning to the breath, letting go of our thoughts, we begin to connect with our basic goodness, which is beyond hope and fear.

The first time a friend discovered he could connect with this idea of basic goodness, this inner luminosity, was when he looked at his daughter. They were sitting at a roadside cafe eating some ice cream and there it was, in her and all around her. She was so innocent and completely engrossed in the experience and taste of the chocolate ice cream. Swirling her spoon in the air, drops of chocolate landing in her hair and on her shirt, but there it was--he could see the light inside her. She had what he had lost so long ago.

If no one has said it yet, getting and/or staying sober is the bravest thing you can do today. What once seemed like the toughest thing imaginable will in fact become "the easier, softer way". You already are that brave, luminous, tender-hearted warrior. You just need to uncover it.

The Meekness of the Tiger

The path of the warrior begins with the Tiger. The meekness of the Tiger is not the fearful scared meekness that first comes to mind. Meek means having a sense of gentleness, genuineness, inquisitiveness and interest (from *The Dignities of Shambhala: A sourcebook*). These are not the qualities of a warrior of aggression, but the qualities of a tender-hearted warrior. Knowing that aggression only brings further suffering, we use these first qualities of bravery to begin our journey.

When we first enter the path of sobriety we will need to have a new sense of gentleness toward ourselves. We have spent countless years being our harshest critics, internally beating ourselves unmercifully. This is a hard habitual pattern to break. We will need to begin with a sense of gentleness toward ourselves, both on and off the cushion. Whenever we lose our breath or have thoughts of picking up, we gently remind ourselves of our purpose and goal. It will may have been a long time since we did even simple activities like going to the supermarket clean and sober. Honestly looking at ourselves is first step in discovering our own genuineness. We begin to discover who we really are, which in the beginning is full of doubt and fear. Most of us will discover we have no idea who we truly are, which is a perfect spot to begin from.

To discover ourselves as we truly are, we need to develop inquisitiveness. When we first get sober we have little idea of who the person before us in the mirror is. What do we like and dislike? What is true and what is false about ourselves are all questions without answers when we first get sober. These questions create an interest in finding out who we are. It is an amazing process, because for many of us it will be the first time we really asked those questions and were interested in the responses. We will also begin to develop an interest in the world around us and in life.

In the early days of sobriety, everything seemed new and foreign. One morning I went to watch a spring training baseball practice. I was amazed at all the people up this early. Nine am on a Saturday morning was still considered early back then, as I had not discovered 6:30am meetings yet. I had no idea what I was really doing there, besides just to see what it was like. Nothing much to do besides sit there in the stands, watching the players run and stretch, laugh and smile, and watch the people around me. Is this what people do on weekends? It was a whole new world. In the last year of my drinking I rarely left the house sober, fearful to get a haircut or go to the mailbox sober. Now, in those first few days and weeks, everything was new and interesting.

The Present Moment

While we were drinking we typically hid in the shadows or stood center stage. Either way we were full of our own self and ego: "look at me" or "I am so bad". The tiger is not that way. The tiger is not trying to show off, nor trying to gain your attention. It is humble and free of arrogance. The beginning of the path contains a sense of the fruition, egolessness. The meekness of the tiger is free of ego. Our egos have caused a great deal of pain. We were unwilling to be open to change or new ways of thinking because we typically thought ourselves the center of the universe. The world should change to meet our needs; we should not have to change to meet the needs of the world. We were unwilling to accept that our way, that our beliefs, were not correct. The tiger is not concerned with itself nor is it fearful of anything. It is content with what it has and where it is. The tiger is content because it knows that everything it needs is contained in the present moment.

Almost all people have difficulty staying in the present moment. When we first begin this journey we are amazed at how much time we spend on either end of the past / future spectrum. You are just like everyone else. Do not beat yourself up over how "unpresent" you are. We all find ourselves trapped in guilt and remorse for the past or anxiety and fear about some unknown future. Our minds constantly travel back and forth between these two places, the past and the future, never resting in the so-called present moment. We need to learn to work with this mind. The tiger embodies present moment awareness; it is fully aware of its mind and body as it moves through the jungle. Yesterday's catch will not keep its belly full today, nor is tomorrow's hunger a concern.

So often these days, we hear the catch-all phrase of "staying in the moment". If I could just "stay in the moment" all shall be well, or so we are told or tell ourselves. We spend so much time and energy worrying about being in the present moment that we miss it. In my opinion, the best we can hope to be is present with our experience of life as it is, not as we wish it was. If we are doing the dishes we can be fully present while doing the dishes. Many times I find myself dealing with my own idea of a situation of who these people are, how I think they will react, how I think they are behaving. I am not actually working with what is going on because I am blocked from being present by my own opinion of what is going on. Sadly, when I was drinking I was not present much and was not working with reality. It can be a beautiful thing to be present for someone. We might actually see them for who they are in that moment.

As near as I can reason, there is no being "in the moment." It is only a purely theoretical place. At least that is how this unenlightened mind feels, which is great because we probably won't get there through reason, intellect or the mind alone. The tiger does not worry about semantics; it is just fully present with its own mind and body. The tiger is genuine and content in the present. It can be present because the tiger is not caught in the suffering of desire of not getting what it wants or rejecting that which it does not like. The tiger works with the world as it is through its meekness. Being present, the tiger can approach the world with the qualities of gentleness, genuineness, interest and inquisitiveness. As the warrior of tiger we can ask, "What does the world have in store right now?" It is for us to discover.

To be comfortable in our own bodies, to be comfortable with the present moment, is the desire of most people, particularly addicts and alcoholics. Understanding that honesty is the key principle of Step One, we can be genuine within our lives and as a result we can begin to honestly see and let go of the states of mind that cause suffering. We are powerless over the people, places and things of the world, but we can approach them without fear. We no longer have to struggle to manage the forces of the world which are unmanageable.

Being brought to our knees, we have become willing to see the world differently. The result is that we are humble and free(er) of arrogance. We have been beaten to a state of willingness and reasonableness. We look around the rooms and see smiling, happy people who all are telling you that they are happy and free because of the steps. Seeing them, you may realize that "maybe" you can do this too. At that moment we have that sense of hope and willingness needed to put our effort to the remainder of the steps.

Step Two

Came to believe that a Power greater than ourselves could restore us to sanity (from Big Book of AA).

When we conclude Step One, what originally seemed like a seemingly hopeless condition begins to have a sense of hope. For the first time in a long time, the sun starts to shine. Step Two seems to many as difficult as Step One. The reason for the difficulty appears, for most people, to center on this concept of believing in a Power greater than ourselves. That capital P smacks you right in the head that the "G" word is coming.

If we have realized how desperate we were in Step One, by getting truly honest about the prospects of a life continued along the path of our addictions, then we may have discovered a willingness to listen to what people in the rooms have to say. Yet so many people run from the prospects of this "Power greater than ourselves" before they give it a fair chance. If you can hold off that vampire in the sunlight reaction, then we can look at the Step in a number of different ways that leave the God question out of the picture, at least for now.

Those who run because of the God question may simply not be ready for sobriety. If you are not "willing to go to any lengths" to remain sober, then you will find a reason why this program cannot work for you, and the God excuse is a very convenient one for many. Are we really willing to keep living in that dark pit of our life because of the word God? The Big Book talks of living by spiritual principles or dying an alcoholic death. Sadly, this is not far from the truth of our life and worse, the alcoholic addict will actually ponder and debate this decision: a different way of life on one hand or an alcoholic death on the other? As the Buddha says, "Suppose a man is struck by a poisoned arrow and the doctor wishes to take out the arrow immediately. Suppose the man does not want the arrow removed until he knows who shot it, his age, his parents, and why he shot it. What would happen? If he were to wait until all these questions have been answered, the man might die first" (from *Zen Keys* by Thich Nhat Hanh). Do we want to be this man? Now that we are dying, whether it be physically or metaphorically, and we are presented a life raft, do we reject the life raft because of what somebody in the raft might believe?

However, if you are truly willing to go to any lengths you will find yourself sticking around for a few meetings. Knowing the true depth of our addictions, the pain of indulging in our addictions will be far greater than the pain of sitting through the occasional Bible thumper.

This Power greater than ourselves does not have to be that celestial being that many of us were told to believe in when we were children. Maybe you were asked to believe in Santa Claus and the Easter Bunny as well? In the end God seemed as real as those two were. Whether we had faith or not while we were drinking, using or abusing, we are not asked or told to follow a particular doctrine in the rooms of Twelve Step recovery. There is no hard and fast line. This power can be anything. In the beginning it is just learning that it was not us. At this point we are not being asked to define or experience anything. You are only asked, "Can you believe in something?"

I have heard all sorts of versions of initial higher powers that people have used: Group Of Drunks, Good Orderly Direction, Grow Or Die, Gift of Desperation, the group, the program, our sponsor-- someone once described his initial higher power as a fat Oprah Winfrey who could hold and soothe him. The point is no one will ask you to fill out an application and judge your higher power. What we are being asked is whether we are willing to believe that we don't need to keep living the way we were living.

Basic Sobriety

Yes We Were Insane

We all long for a relief from suffering. Sadly, no matter what we do that relief is generally short-lived. Step One showed us that we were all suffering, through our powerlessness and unmanageable lives. We need to see how bad things were so that we can see hope, the possibility for a different way of life.

"...if we be alcoholic we are caught in a trap we cannot spring. We have to have help, and we can't get it until we recognize the need for it." (*A New Pair of Glasses* by Chuck C.)

We need to recognize and understand that the patterns of our lives, our ways of thinking, were in essence insane. Powerlessness and unmanageability had us over the barrel and if we went no further we would gladly get in the barrel, throw up our hands in despair, and let the barrel go over the falls. Taking a good, deep look we saw how truly powerless and unmanageable our lives had been. We must have been insane not to see it. Could we have been anything other than insane not to see it? This is where our hope begins. Once we can see the insanity of our thinking, we immediately give birth to the hope that we can be restored to sanity. Extrapolating something the Sakyong wrote in the Shambhala Sadhana, one could say that even at the razor's edge of insanity, sanity always exists.[13]

Dawn of Hope

Just by walking through the door into a meeting, or not picking up for 24 hours, you believe in something. You believed that maybe, just maybe, this might work. This is the spark of hope. It may not seem it yet, because we don't have a complete faith yet, but a hope in the possibility of our own sobriety. There is a belief that there may be something better than the life we have been living. The

---

[13] Original quote: "But even at the razor's edge of unenlightened society, enlightened society always exists." from the *Shambhala Sadhana* by Sakyong Mipham

definition of the word "believe" is to "have confidence in the truth of something, although without absolute proof" (Dictionary.com). True, there is no magic pill or silver bullet when it comes to sobriety. Nothing is 100% guaranteed and provable about anyone's sobriety. Yet at this stage of the steps we do have a bit of tangible evidence. Most of us are so skeptical of this whole thing working, that there is any way out of the darkness, that we even doubt that the people around us at meetings are sober. Aren't they as obsessed about alcohol, sex and drugs as we are? However, when we open our eyes and really look around the room, we see that people are indeed sober, at least for today.

We come to believe that change is possible.

My Own Spark of Hope

I did not get sober in a rehab or a detox. I had convinced myself for years that it was much more important for me to earn a paycheck than it was to go to rehab for a 30-day "vacation". That by my own willpower I could rein in my drinking. Then, when I was unemployed for 16 months, I had convinced myself I could not afford rehab. What I really meant was that I could not imagine any other way to get through a day than getting drunk. I did not want to quit drinking. Unemployment gave me a plethora of excuses for getting drunk after a hard day of being a stay-at-home dad. When I was working again, I struggled each day to not get drunk after I left the office. Hungover and possibly still drunk every morning did not make me a model employee. When I reached the breaking point between drinking and living, I was terrified that taking a 30-day sabbatical for rehab possibly meant losing my job. The result was that my early days of sobriety were spent at my desk in an office cubicle. At least my cubicle was in the back rear corner of the office. This way no one heard when my head hit my desk or I fell out of my chair when it got near five o'clock and that wave of desire would arise. For a while, the desire was so strong that it would knock me over - literally, *thump*.

In the beginning the desire for alcohol was my constant companion. Thankfully, hand-in-hand with that desire was an equally strong fear of not being able to stop if I started drinking again. I was no longer afraid of just losing one night to drinking; if I picked up I knew it meant weeks and months of a return to that darkness. When I began my life in AA, I did not tell most of the people close to me, i.e., my family, that I had stopped drinking and had started to attend AA meetings for fear that it would not work for me. While the Big Book may start the chapter on How it Works with as positive a statement as you can get--"Rarely have we seen a person fail who has thoroughly followed our path"--it then follows it with "Those who do not recover..." (Big Book of AA). This was not a sure thing. In fact, the more I researched the more I discovered that the odds were distinctly not in my favor. For every three of us who get and remain sober, ninety-seven others are still struggling, drinking and dying.

It was the morning of day fifteen where I first felt that spark of hope. Waking for work that morning, I took a shower (a new concept in sobriety, showering before work) when it hit me that it was day fifteen. At the end of my drinking I could not go fifteen minutes by myself and not be drinking, so the realization that I was at day fifteen amazed me. The spark of "maybe this could really work for me" began.

Before getting sober, I believe that the longest I ever went without drinking in the previous twenty one years was twenty-one days, which I managed twice. The first time I managed about twenty-one days was when I found a strange bite on my shoulder. The next day it was worse so I went to the doctor. They immediately prescribed 30 days of hardcore antibiotics, the kind used to fight malaria, as they suspected it to be a Lyme-carrying tick bite. Faced with the prospects of a lifelong painful disease or thirty days sober, I immediately called in sick and got drunk for two days straight before starting the medicine. Luckily, the bite bull's-eyed shortly after I had started the medicine. I stayed miserably dry for about twenty-one days before I figured I was out of danger and therefore rationalized drinking again as long as I kept taking the antibiotic. Thankfully the Lyme never got a hold in my system and the antibiotics worked. That was as close to some form of sobriety as I would come for quite some time. I would occasionally stop drinking for a few days at the "request" of wife #2. Fortunately for me, and unfortunately for her, all I needed to do was wait a few days, knowing she would call me at work saying to bring something to drink home for her, which gave me the green light and off I would go again. This continued for a few years, until she reached her breaking point and was done. At the end we were living in the same house only for our daughter's sake. With a last-ditch effort I white knuckled some sobriety with the express purpose of trying to get her to stay. I did not want to be sober, but I knew I was about 5 feet over the "she's going to leave" line and the co-dependent in me was desperately trying to get back on the other side. I made it through three tortuous weeks. Being dry is not the same as being sober. During those three weeks, even though I was not drinking my character defects remained, i.e., I was not a happy camper. In fact, I was infinitely more irritable because I really did not want to be sober and hated every moment of being dry. As a result she still left and I celebrated the end of another long-term relationship and another daughter living in two households by cracking a beer and putting an end to my sobriety for the next year. With no one around to pretend to keep my drinking in check for, I quickly spiraled further and further into darkness.

So that realization at fifteen days of sobriety came with a wonderful feeling of hope, a belief that maybe this could work. Maybe even I, who had absolutely "no willpower," might be able to get this. I was beginning to learn to trust sobriety, my sponsor and the program. I had no idea why this stuff was working, but there I was sober. By allowing myself the space and time to be in the world without mind-altering substances, I had begun to develop some trust and faith in reality. I had discovered some hope. I was experiencing the world as it was, the good and the bad. It was still pretty terrifying most days, but to quote an anonymous friend, "It didn't eat me."

Basic Sobriety

The world has been sending us signals from the very beginning; my addiction took me further and further from that wisdom. Easing into this experience of trust, I began to approach the world as it is, letting go of the fight and struggle for it to be other than it is. Day by day, faith in reality grew. I began to believe and trust in reality and my sobriety. I began to hope and believe that I could be in the world without drugs or alcohol. I was learning to be genuine. At fifteen days, I did not understand all that was happening or the deeper meaning embedded in those first two weeks, but what I did know was that somehow this stuff was working. I was sober and that alone was incredible.

The Cocoon

We are all born with a natural basic sanity. This is our essence, this brilliant luminosity which is at the beginning at our core that we are basically sane. Our basic sanity is open and natural, free from constraints and constructs. Unfortunately, with that innate openness comes a sense of rawness which is unprotected and open to be hurt. To keep from being hurt, we have created layer over layer of physical, mental and emotional habits to hide and protect our basic sanity. The result is that we buried our natural, innate sanity deep inside, far removed from the dangers of the world. What we created to be our protection from the world is metaphorically a cocoon. The thread of this cocoon is so fine that we did not realize that we were binding ourselves up in it. What we created in the cocoon was our little sanctuary from the world, a sanctuary from all the people and pain the world caused us. We closed all the doors and windows, filled all the gaps and cracks, so that nothing new and fresh could reach us. As a result, over time our cocoon became smelly and stinky, but because it was our cocoon we did not even notice how bad it was. We were completely cut off from the world, safe in our cocoons. The cocoon is our neurotic habits and neuroses which we used to protect ourselves from the world. The cocoon is our insanity.

How the Cocoon Grows

Each step along the path of addiction toward insanity was incremental. Little by little the addiction was growing as other forces tried to keep everything in control. Just as our addiction grew little by little, so did our cocoon, from the moment of birth. The cocoon kept us from truly experiencing the world. The cocoon keeps us from our basic sanity. Once it is discovered that the cocoon exists, the hope arises that it can be taken apart. There is a way out of the cocoon. There is a hope of a life outside the cocoon--a life outside of our insanity and addiction.

Our cocoon is created by the habitual patterns that we continued to repeat over and over again. In Twelve Step parlance that is the definition of insanity that Step Two refers to. Even though these patterns or behaviors are detrimental to us, we continue to repeat them. While we may have wanted the results to be different, deep inside we knew the results would be the same. We wanted the oblivion, the ease and comfort that we hoped would come from acting in our addiction. We just did not want the inevitable train wreck, guilt and remorse that came with it. The result we wanted was for the pain to end and we only knew one way to do that-- through our addiction. Our starting point was good, human and natural; we wanted to avoid the suffering we felt. In our addictions we were not experiencing life as it really was, but life as we hoped it would be. Maybe we got a moment of relief, but we could never stop at that point, and then we woke to remorse and guilt. Whatever caused yesterday's pain still had to be dealt with. Therefore another drink sounded like a good idea. Rinse and repeat for best results, right?

As Jon Kabat-Zin says in *Full Catastrophe Living; Yet some people try to avoid stress by walling themselves off from life experience; others attempt to anesthetize themselves one way or another to escape it. Of course, it is only sensible to avoid undergoing unnecessary pain and hardship... But if escape and avoidance become our habitual ways of dealing with our problems, problems just multiply. They don't magically go away. What does go away or gets covered over when we tune out our problems, run away from them, or simply go numb is our power to continue to learn and grow to change and to heal. When it comes right down to it, facing our problems is usually the only way to get past them.*

Great Eastern Sun

Within the Shambhala tradition the greatest symbol of hope is the Great Eastern Sun. It is the light outside the cocoon. The Great Eastern Sun is a symbol of the guiding light of Basic Goodness and ultimately the freedom from the cocoon of habitual patterns. This sun is always there, regardless of the weather or our moods. It shines in the darkness like the earth's sun shines in space, always there regardless of day and night, constant. Our position and the clouds may block the sun's rays but it is always there. The Great Eastern Sun is the sun of mid-morning; the new day has dawned and we are moving forward into that new day. It is a rising sun which embodies a feeling of hope and possibility. These feelings of hope and possibility give us a sense of upliftedness. It is Great because it always exists, beyond space and time, beyond good and bad; the Great Eastern Sun exists and we can sense its radiance. Typically we turn from that radiance, but now we are beginning to get the sense that the cocoon is not the way life should be. The Great Eastern Sun shines on the actual world, illuminating things as they are and not how we wish them to be. We begin to sense that we could actually live in the world. We are moving forward toward genuineness and sanity.

The Great Eastern Sun is a "power greater than ourselves" that we begin to experience as we are breaking out of our cocoon. Once we realize that we are trapped in this cocoon a sense of claustrophobia and panic occurs. We want out! Yet we also really like it there. These two feelings, of comfort and claustrophobia, fight each other. We find we can't breathe and so we start tearing at the walls of the cocoon to let in air and light, but just a little bit at first--just enough to get a little bit of fresh air in. From inside the cocoon, what is outside the cocoon is marvelous and mysterious. What is outside is also terrifying and frightening. In the beginning we are only peeking out of the cocoon. That first whiff of fresh air we experience is the experience of basic goodness. The light outside the cocoon is the light of the Great Eastern Sun. That light shines on the possibility of freedom outside the cocoon, the freedom of being an awake human being.

Hope always lies before us when we choose to see the possibility of doing something different than we have always done before. The feeling of the Great Eastern Sun is akin to the phrase in recovery, "You can restart your day at any time." No matter how bad the day, we can pause, take a breath, call someone or go to a meeting, and we can begin the day anew. We don't have to keep riding the wave of our day; we can get off and change direction at any time. Let me repeat that statement again: we can change our direction at any time. We can play the tape forward, let it go, and have a fresh start. You do not always need to yell when you stub your toe. You do not always need to eat a turkey sandwich at the deli. You do not have to inflict pain for the pain others cause you. Each moment is a choice. Each moment is connected to the one before it, but completely whole, fresh and new. This allows us to break our insanity and move forward in a different, saner way.

In recovery we cannot rest on our laurels; we must continue to move forward each day. It may be just one day at a time. You can drink tomorrow. You can always drink tomorrow, but if played right, that tomorrow never comes. That is the Great Eastern Sun in action. It is always there, leading us forward. No matter how much we want to give in or how tired we are, it is still there. The Great Eastern Sun is always there to remind us where we are heading and light our way.

Basic Sobriety

Basic Sanity

What is it that the Great eastern Sun illuminates? At this stage we just have the first glimpses of the Great Eastern Sun, but it is enough for us to begin to believe, to hope. We have a little taste of that freedom and that is enough to keep us progressing to open the cocoon more and more. We discover the idea of Basic Goodness and we have a belief that our basic sanity lies further on ahead. Basic sanity is natural to all of us. It is our fundamental way of existing. It is open, free space. "Basic sanity can be described as a state of mind which, through the absence of hope and fear, rests in unencumbered openness" (*Recalling Chogyam Trungpa* by Traleg Kyabgon). The cocoon is the opposite. The cocoon is the insanity of the Second Step. Staying within the cocoon is the desire to stay in the world of what Chogyam Trungpa coined the setting sun, not the open, free world of the Great Eastern Sun we sense outside the cocoon. The setting sun world is the world we are afraid to face. It is the world of mind-numbing ignorance and avoidance. The setting sun world is dressed up in pretty sparkly dresses and tells you that if you buy the next iPhone you will finally feel ok. The setting sun world is where happiness is always just around the corner. It is the world we knew, the one of darkness and despair, and we never have to go back there again.

Once we take our seat and begin the practice of meditation, we learn to touch our genuine nature, which is our basic sanity. Thus our true nature is a sane one. When we are sitting everything comes up--our likes and dislikes, our hopes and fears--just as they are and maybe not as we would like them to be. We acknowledge the thoughts then let them go. This letting go is how we begin to discover our genuineness and through that genuineness we begin to discover our authentic presence, our genuine self. Here at Step Two we are just at the beginning of that journey to authentic presence, which starts from simply letting go. We begin with letting go our addiction and the comfort of the cocoon. We start by letting go of anything that gets in the way of escaping our addiction and the cocoon, absurd as that may seem. Each time we want to pull the covers over our heads and hide, we let go of the story and move through the fear.

In the beginning everything seems fearful. We addicts and alcoholics have made mountains out molehills for a long time. We will discover so many things along the way that will try to bring us back into the cocoon, that setting sun way of thinking, and we will need to continue to let go of them. Giving up the fight was our key to the new beginning in Step One; now because we believe we can change, we can let go of some of our old ideas and stories. As the Big Book reminds us, "Some of us have tried to hold on to our old ideas and the result was nil until we let go absolutely" (Big Book of AA).

Relaxing into the Tiger

The Tiger embodies genuineness. A tiger does not pretend to be something it is not. He does not put on airs. He is not arrogant, nor timid. He is simply a tiger. He is a balanced combination of self-satisfaction and modesty. He is relaxed and comfortable in his own skin. As the tiger walks through the jungle he is not worried about past triumphs or failures. He is not preoccupied and anxious about the future. The tiger walks with genuineness because he is fully aware of karma so each step is one of mindfulness and awareness. The warrior of meekness can walk through the world with genuineness.

Through the sitting practice of meditation we have begun to see the confines of the cocoon and have discovered the feeling of something existing beyond the cocoon. As we begin to relax into ourselves, letting go of the habitual thoughts and patterns, we begin to develop genuineness. Genuineness may seem startling at times as we discover new things about ourselves. We may realize that we really don't like the things we pretended to have interest in before or we may allow ourselves the freedom to enjoy things that we once derided as stupid. As the Sakyong mentions, humanity is always trying to answer "Who am I?" and now we are beginning to ask and answer that question for ourselves.

Books, Books and More Books

When I moved in with my now wife, I had a very large personal book collection, amassed over the course of more than two decades. At the end of my first marriage, I used books to numb my brain. I could not tell myself stories about my own life when I was pumping it full of other stories, typically reading 500 plus pages a day. In sobriety I didn't have the hunger I once had hunting for new books. That obsessive-compulsive need to find the next great hidden gem seemed to fade. So I made a decision to part with many of the books. This meant that I had to go through each book one by one and ask myself why I bought the book. Was this book bought because I wanted to be the guy who had books like these, the classic century old obscure authors that no one else knew? Was I holding on to them merely because I have OCD about collecting stuff? Turned out that I did not really like many of the books I had carried with me on dozens of moves around the country. When I began the paring down process I had a few thousand books and that number is now down to less than one hundred. Most of the ones I have kept are because I truly enjoyed them, not because I want you to think I enjoy them, although there are probably a few ego-feeding books still hiding in there waiting to be cut out.

Everything is Workable

Going through life sober, while awkward at first, is infinitely saner than our drinking life. It may still be quite foggy in early sobriety but somewhere in there we become aware of our basic sanity. The more we start to experience our basic sanity the less of our neurotic pain we feel over time. In the beginning, it may feel like we are experiencing more neurotic pain, but that is only because we have started to have some clarity of mind for the first time, therefore we experience it more directly.

We can begin to feel powerful like the tiger. As we grow in that feeling, we can begin to relax more with the world. As a warrior of tiger we start to see that there are no problems, or as they like to say in the rooms of recovery "only possibilities." We have no inherent problems because everything is workable. Seeing the world more directly, without the stories of our cocoons, seeing it without filters, we see the truth of the world being workable. We know that our actions will continue to have karmic results, so we aim our intentions toward positive growth.

"Progress not perfection," as the Big Book says. When we take a moment and see how far we have come, we experience a sense of joy. Just getting to this point in our sobriety is momentous. We have started to make progress. We may not see it yet but it is there. Others, outside of the rooms, will not generally understand what an achievement our sobriety is. They can pick up alcohol, or other substances, and put them down with ease. The Big Book describes how without "an entire psychic change there is little hope of his recovery."[14] Nothing can have the desired effect on an alcoholic to stop their drinking. Those are pretty dramatic words. Connecting with our basic sanity through the sitting practice of meditation and the warriorship of Shambhala is how we bolster that process of an "entire psychic change" within us.

The initial fog has started to lift, and while we may have a great deal of heavy lifting ahead of us, that inner feeling of strength and goodness is starting to grow. That strength needs to be nurtured and cultivated. We are beginning to truly feel the power of the tiger. We are becoming a warrior in the world.

We come to believe that our course of action, sobriety and meditation, will lead us to further uncover our basic sanity. We can in fact return to the state of mind that existed before our neuroses took over. It has always existed within us, we just have to uncover it.

---

[14] Doctor's Opinion from the Big Book of AA, p. XXIX.

Basic Sobriety

It is the Buddha nature mind and the mind of basic goodness that exists within all of us. Uncovering this basic sanity will allow for that "We will intuitively know how to handle situations that used to baffle us" (Big Book of AA) fruition down the road. When we uncover our basic sanity we will work with situations as they are directly, not how we want them to be.

Power to Keep Going

It seems that each step will ask us to do or come to understand a concept that, at our initial impression, will seem terrifying. It may be a Power greater than ourselves, God, the fearless inventory, telling another being, and the list goes on, which is why the Big Book states "if you want what we have." We are going to have to want it. This will be new territory and that new territory will seem impossible. This is why hope is so important at this stage, because we hope that to do these actions will relieve us of our addiction. All of these actions and beliefs are well outside our cocoons and we surely wouldn't do them if our very life was not at stake. The truth is our addictions were killing us. The cocoon was killing us. Looking back at this point, we may have already started to taste basic goodness, to feel its fresh air. The horrors of the past may have started to fade and there will be the thought, *Oh, it wasn't that bad.* It usually did not take much to push us to drinking before to run back into that setting sun world. We drank over sorrows and over joys. We drank because the sun was out or because it rained. Maybe you will believe yourself when your ego tries to coax you back into the cocoon. Which lie will it be? It is when we see clearly that our pasts were honestly as bad as and probably a lot worse than we realized that our journey out of the cocoon begins.

The growth of the Steps, out of the cocoon, will at times be painful because "all we have to change is everything," as my sponsor would remind me in the early days. He would follow it up with the promise of joy as the result of a life lived one hundred and eighty degrees different from the way I had been living. Sakyong Mipham Rinpoche talks about how all we need to make a change is ten percent. We do not need to change all at once, we just need to start the movement going. If we can change little by little, we can make this seemingly huge turn-around by beginning little by little. Each of the steps is a little bit more of that change. To open the door to that path, we just have to believe that it is possible to change. That is all that is asked of us today in Step Two: to believe that change is possible. We believe that through sobriety and meditation we may discover our basic sanity.

Once that door is open, we move through to Step Three.

Step Three

Made a decision to turn our will and our lives over to the care of God as we understood him. (Big Book of AA)

There it is, right? The God word? Don't go running away just yet. Many newcomers see that word and head for the door without giving sobriety a chance. Many will see that word and it will keep them from sobriety, thinking that the only way to participate in any Twelve Step program is to believe in a singular, almighty creator. Even in the 1930s there was enough of a dissension among the ranks for them to add the supremely powerful clause "as we understood him". This gives us the wiggle room we need to sit back down in our chairs. Whether we look at it from a theistic point of view, a non-theistic point of view, or somewhere in between, we can find a great deal of value in this step to aid our recovery.

Before we get into the big questions about God and higher powers, I'd like to start with a simpler look at this step. The first time I went through this step I knew I could not wrap myself around the higher power idea just yet. My mind was still very cloudy at that time, so grandiose debates about God and the nature of the universe would have to wait. My foothold through this step was "my will".

Self Will Run Riot

Having thought I was basically the center of my own universe for the last twenty years, I thought the universe existed solely to make me happy. Of course, the universe doesn't work that way. In fact I was probably on the edge of insanity most of the time. I had this view of myself as intelligent (overly so), creative, sensitive and caring, yet for some reason the universe did not unfold the way I thought it should for a person of my ability and upstanding character. The universe was behaving the way it was, the girlfriend and the ex-wife were behaving the way they were, the economy and everything else was happening the way it should. I just could not see or accept it, so I continued to get drunk every evening and was dumbfounded that the world kept kicking me in the shins. Only when I was brought to the edge of the abyss by alcoholism did I become willing to believe that maybe there was another way.

When it came time to do the Third Step, I was beginning to see and understand the insanity of my drinking life. More shall be revealed and now, as the veil was beginning to lift, I could see some of my past behaviors from a completely different perspective. My image of myself and the reality of myself were drastically opposed to one another. "I was drunk at the time" was a flimsy excuse for how my morals dropped while acting in my ism. My behaviors were not consistent with who I thought I was.

So if I was not who I thought I was when I was drinking, then who was I? More importantly, if I was not acting out "my will" when drinking, then whose will was I acting out? The image I held of myself was that I was a caring, hardworking and fun-loving guy, a devoted husband and father. When I became honest about who I really was, particularly while drinking, I discovered that that was not even remotely true. In fact the countless letters and emails I had from my two ex-wives showed me that I distinctively was not the so-called person I thought I had been.

The realization that my behaviors and actions did not match who I thought I was ended my initial debate. When I asked myself how I could have been and done those things, I discovered that I was completely mistaken about "my will." I had given up my will long ago. I had given it to Budweiser and Jack Daniels. When I started drinking, or needed to drink, I would do all sorts of things I never would have thought I would do, including stealing from my own children's piggy banks if they had any money when my own funds were being policed. There are a handful of behaviors that while sober I would not even contemplate, but I did while drunk or dry and yep, I have the tape to prove it.

Basic Sobriety

For all of us, the day came when there was no longer a choice; we had to use. Having given our will and our lives over to our addiction, in utter desperation, we looked for another way. In Narcotics Anonymous, we decided to turn our will and our lives over to the care of God as we understand him. (NA Basic Text)

It didn't really matter at first which God I was going to give my will to. I didn't have one to give. I had given it to my addiction. It was irrelevant whether I gave it to a Christian God, a Jewish God, a Group of Drunks, or the table. I could no longer quibble about my precious will. My will was the way of alcohol and that was not a pretty picture. Anything had to be better than that. For those first few months of recovery, my higher power was my sponsor, the program and the fellowship of AA. It was certainly no longer me.

The great "I" was done for and that is the most important element of this step. This is the call of the Third Step--that we are giving up our attempts to control our lives and the world around us. This is where we pause, catching ourselves "taking our will back" when we are trying to scheme, manipulate, or control. It is up to us to take the actions, but the results we leave alone. Ever go bowling, trying with all your might to control the ball after it has left your hand? In Step Three we must learn that we have no control after we let the ball go. Whatever happens after that point--strike, gutter, or split--that is what we have to work with next.

Seeking a Higher Power

Now, please don't think once I loop-holed my way through the Step I was done with it. Looking around the rooms I knew there had to be something to this God thing. At the end of the "How it Works" reading from chapter 5 of the Big Book, were the ABC's:

a) *That we were alcoholic and could not manage our own lives.*
b) *That probably no human power could have relieved our alcoholism.*

c)   That God could and would if he were sought.

So I did. I sought because "to be doomed an alcoholic death or to live on a spiritual basis are not always easy alternatives to face" (from The Big Book of AA). I knew I was beat. So I became a seeker. That story is told in the introduction so I won't tell it again. If you did the typical alcoholic thing and jumped right in and skipped the introduction, you can go back now.

As the 12 & 12 says, "Fortunately, we who have tried it, and with equal misgivings, can testify that anyone, anyone at all, can begin to do it. We can further add that a beginning, even the smallest, is all that is needed. Once we have placed the key of willingness in the lock and have the door ever so slightly open, we find we can always open it some more,"   and thus this was the beginning; the door was open a crack and that was enough to push through into the step.

"God as we understood him" gives us a lot of leeway in creating our own version of a higher power or power greater than ourselves. Even though we are working from a non-theistic base in Buddhism, in general, and Shambhala, in particular, there are a number of options that fall within the "power greater than ourselves" category. In my pre-sobriety studies during college of Buddhism, I fixated on the concept of dissolving the boundary between self and other, that all is "emptiness." In my simplistic mind it meant that there was no difference between inside and outside, that there was nothing inside here; therefore there was no "God out there". This did not bode well for my understanding in the early stages of sobriety and study of a power greater than myself. However, in the early days of sobriety, in those moments when there is no one between you and opening the liquor store door, I believe that it is vitally important to identify with a power greater than ourselves.

Concepts of Powers Greater Than Ourselves

The world is an extraordinary place. We have been shut off from its majesty and beauty through our addiction. The cracks in our cocoon are letting in the light of the Great Eastern Sun to draw us forward. The vulnerability we once shut ourselves off from now starts to show around the edges. There is the moment where the cocoon calls us and we know we cannot go back into our cocoon. We must stay open and available to the world. The question is how?

In my first week of meetings a fellow picked up a chip celebrating his 27th year of sobriety. The tradition is to ask the person how many and how did they do it. Given the floor, he described how the faith he had at the beginning of his sobriety was so primitive, a simple structure of rocks and twigs. Over time he kept adding to it, knocking down a wall here, rebuilding over there. Today his faith still keeps some of the simplicity of his original faith with a quarter century of spiritual searching added on. His faith has grown, changed and developed over time.

That simple rock structure of faith began to take a form inside myself in the meditation hall. I would look around the meditation hall at our center and see the faces of Chogyam Trungpa Rinpoche and his son, the current lineage holder, Sakyong Mipham Rinpoche. Their pictures were on each side of the Rigden thanka. A thanka is a traditional painting form usually depicting a Buddhist deity or scene. The scenes may depict the Buddha, important Lamas, bodhisattvas or teachers, much the way paintings of Jesus, the apostles and other saints are used in Christianity.

My faith in these people and teachings grew to form a tangible seed. Some of the people at our center had been students of Chogyam Trungpa since the early days of the 1970s. They showed me what the teachings looked like in action, much the way we look to the old timers in the rooms of recovery. If I did what they did, then maybe I would have similar results. The writings of Trungpa and his son provided the nourishment for the seeds of faith to grow. To see what they had discovered, realized and understand about themselves and the world around them. They were part of a lineage, a long line of teachers that stretched all the way back to the Buddha. This lineage also consisted of enlightened rulers and people regardless of their spiritual pedigree, men and women committed to trying to make the world a better place.

This is faith based on proof. Does the teaching provide results? If not discard it and continue searching. This is not faith based on believing because someone else believes. Tangible evidence of the validity of the teachings was both visible in the people around me, but also through my own experience. I could feel and taste the validity of the teachings for myself.

These elements of the teachers, writings and fellow travelers on the path are representative of what Buddhists term the Three Jewels. The Three Jewels consist of the Buddha, the dharma and the sangha. A person could take refuge as a sign of faith outwardly, a vow, or inwardly as an act of faith in the Three Jewels. One could take refuge in the Buddha as a man, not a God, who discovered his true nature and became enlightened. The Buddha is represented by and in all the teachers and everyone around us. The dharma is represented by the words of the Buddha, the writings and teachings. Those fellow travelers, the fellowship, are what constitute the sangha. They are the ones who constantly teach us on the path.

Buddha is not a God. Chogyam Trungpa is not a God. The Sakyong is not a God. They are ordinary people who connected with their basic goodness and developed true understanding about themselves. They were not different, fundamentally, than you or I. It is only our egos that tell us that they are different from us, that they are over there being all realized and we are over here banging our heads against the wall. The inner teaching about the powers greater than ourselves is that we are not separate from them. It is only our concepts and own mind that make it appear as if they are separate from us. When we ask for help from the Buddha or any other enlightened teacher or deity (a god in a polytheistic religion), what we are doing since they are not separate from us is merely tapping into a part of ourselves that we are disconnected from at the moment. We are not asking for something outside of ourselves to come and give us something we did not already have. We have merely lost our connection to our innate patience, or compassion, or generosity.

We begin to emulate the Buddha by sitting down and meditating. When we meditate we connect with the same essence and qualities that the Buddha and other realized teachers have discovered. What we discover is that everything we need is already within us.

If we get out of our own way enough, unwrap the cocoon, we already have it (enlightenment, Buddha nature, Basic Goodness, etc.) within us. Or to say it another way, "The kingdom of God is within you." We develop faith in the path of discovering our own true nature. Enlightenment is always possible in each and every one of us. When we sit down and meditate we are beginning to connect with powers greater than the self we think we are. We touch our basic goodness and feel the strength created by having what Trungpa liked to call "good head and shoulders." The first moments of this happen as if by accident, but we know that it is there and so we make a decision to continue the path of discovery.

We all have the possibility of becoming Buddha. If we follow the Buddha's example, follow his lead, we will discover that there is no difference between us and him. There is no separation between us and anyone. When we truly see this we will see the nature of all things including our own true nature. We see the Buddha within ourselves and everyone else. This is what we aspire to when we take refuge in the Buddha. This is the essence of turning it over and getting out of our own way to allow this higher power within us to emerge.

Confidence

Once we have taken refuge, placing our faith in the Buddha, dharma and sangha, we develop a sense of confidence. Taking refuge and making the decision to be in the world as it is takes confidence. Even if we do not take refuge, we can still make this decision to be in the world as it is. The Shambhala path of working with the dignities does not require you to take refuge or necessarily let go of your prior spiritual or religious beliefs. It is simply making a commitment, making a decision, to be present in the world at each moment. In the Shambhala lineage this is called the birth of the warrior. The warrior does not go roaring off into the world, causing destruction in his wake; the ignorant and barbaric do that. No, this is the bravery of the warrior who is willing to deal with the world as it is and not how he wishes it to be. Taking refuge gives us the faith and confidence that we can continue our journey into the world. We have begun to see the Basic Goodness in the world outside the cocoon. We are willing to explore the world with confidence. This confidence comes from knowing that we have everything we already need.

As we develop confidence in our self, in trusting our inner peace, we let go of our aggression. Without our aggression we can face the world and our fears. We aim our actions to best be in accord with the laws of karma and the teachings of the dharma. We no longer need to use our aggression to battle the world. We can use discernment and confidence to steer us through the world. With our confidence we no longer struggle with the way the world is. Each moment becomes a decision to step farther into the world, to not return to our cocoon. As confidence grows we see the cocoon for what it was. Free from the cocoon, this world is fresh and wonderful.

Every moment has everything we need. We do not need to ask for someone else to take care of things for us. Relying on the world and the power of our confidence in our Basic Goodness creates faith that we can work with the world, that we will not be overwhelmed. As we drop our fear and doubt we become gentler and more relaxed. When we become gentler with ourselves, we can extend that gentleness to the world around us. It is as the third step prayer reminds us that "victory over them [difficulties] may bear witness to those I would help." This lack of aggression with ourselves and the world is the fruition of the tiger. The tiger has confidence as it walks through the jungle. No step is a mistake; no motion is in error. Within the warrior it comes from making a decision to believe in the Basic Goodness of the world, from taking refuge in the Buddha, dharma, and sangha, and the decision to free ourselves of our habitual patterns and cocoon.

Working with the world as it is is very powerful. Each morning we wake and make the decision to work with the world in this way. If we falter we have the strength of the three jewels to remind us of the strength we have within us. Around us are the fellowship and the decision to continue with the steps. Step Three at its core is simply making this decision, to go forward into the world and to continue with the Steps. When we reach this point in the steps, we have confidence in the power of our own sobriety, what I like to call the fourth jewel. Having a few twenty-four hours under our belt, we have surely come across moments of fear and anxiety. Relying on all our tools, we can continue to walk through those fears. We expand our faith in our own Basic Goodness and learn to trust ourselves and the process.

A Story of Faith

A member of our recovery group, Roger, a landscape designer, described to me an extremely traumatic event and time where his faith was not only tested but confirmed.

One Friday morning around ten, I got a text message from my son's mother to call her, as she had something important to discuss. As I was leaving shortly for a weekend retreat on the other coast of Florida, I called her right away and asked her to tell me what it was since we would not be able to discuss it in person for a few days. The response I got came completely out of left field, as she said, "I got engaged last week and will be moving with the kids (her daughter from her first marriage and our son) to Pennsylvania to live with him."

This completely took me by surprise. I expressed that I did not agree with her taking our son and made some suggestions like her going up there, getting settled and then sending for our son. She didn't see things the way I was seeing them. In fact she started to rant and scream about "not being allowed to get on with her life." I knew we were not going to agree at that moment so I did what I was taught to do. I punted and paused the discussion till I returned from the retreat.

The drive across the state allowed my new wife and me plenty of time to discuss our options. What were our options? Let her leave with our son into a situation we knew nothing about and hope that everything worked out fine for our son or fight for him to remain with us. What would "God's will" be for our child? If we let him go and the fiancé turned out to be a child molester, how could we look at our child and say we did nothing, letting it be in God's hands so to speak? Our decision was that we would fight because we felt it was in his best interest to stay with us. If the universe determined otherwise we would accept that and have faith that the outcome was the right one, regardless if we won or lost.

A friend in the rooms advised me to get my ex's plans because I did not have the slightest idea what she was thinking. He suggested a polite email expressing my regret for not being happier when we talked, about her finding a new love, and asking if she could let me know what her plan was. At the same time we reached out to a few friends in the rooms who had used a family lawyer and a few recommended the same one. When my ex returned my email Sunday afternoon, it basically stated that since she was currently unemployed and living on her parent's couch with all of her and the kids stuff in storage it would be pretty simple to just pick up and go, but she was still debating about whether to go over the Christmas break or sooner.

Not having technically been married to this person, we never needed a divorce. Up until then we had been living with a makeshift parenting plan, where we had tried to maintain 50/50 custody. For the years after we broke up I was terrified of what would have happened if we went to the courts.

Basic Sobriety

Now, with our backs against the wall, we were going to ask the courts to give me, the father and a recovering alcoholic, primary custody of our son.

With her email in hand I went to see the lawyer first thing Monday morning. We talked for a little bit about the situation and about my alcoholic past. The lawyer recommended that we act quickly. The email response to the "what's your plan" inquiry was the basis of what would become an emergency injunction to bind our son to the county until such time as the court could decide what was best.

Miraculously, 24 hours after seeing the lawyer and telling her the case, we had the papers in hand. The lawyer was amazed and grateful that the papers got through the system so quickly. When I asked my ex if we could meet later to talk about things, i.e., serve her the papers, the response I got was "I can't; we are packed and leaving."

BAM! Even today, my blood pressure drops remembering that moment when I read her text. I was floored. As best I could, I started calling my network. Words didn't work so well, as my crying made the words illegible, so I started texted people. I managed to call the lawyer and told her what was happening. She told me to hang tight; that she would see what she could do, as well as begin preparation for issuing an Amber Alert (abducted child alert). Knowing I couldn't go back to work, I headed over to the AA clubhouse near my office. There is a saying: "If your ass falls off, you pick up your ass and get to a meeting." I was going to be an hour early for the noon meeting but I knew it would be the best place for me to be. Going to the clubhouse would be better than going to a bar. On the way to the clubhouse, my lawyer called outlining a Hail Mary plan to cut them off as they were leaving.

At the lawyer's office, the plan was to have the process server follow me in his car and see if we could locate her. Our first stop was to be my son's maternal grandparents' house, hoping that she would stop there on her way out of town. If that did not work then we would head to where I believed where my ex had been living for the past few weeks. I also sent her a text message asking if I could at least say goodbye to my son. Twenty minutes later, she responded, "Of course you can say goodbye." We agreed to meet nearby at a local big box store, where we had done drop-offs in the past, so we both knew where to look for each other in the parking lot. She would be there in fifteen minutes, she said.

The process server and I headed to the parking lot, where I sat under a small tree and he parked a few aisles away. The basic plan was that as soon as my son was in my arms, he was to serve her the papers. I sat and sat, working with all the crazy emotions in me. I did not have a clue as to what was going to happen when she showed up, but I continued to have faith that whatever was supposed to happen would happen. Friends from the program kept calling as time passed. One friend asked, "Is your son to leave with her or with you?" That was a really good question. I had no idea what was supposed to happen after she was served with the papers. So I called the lawyer and the lawyer said that the papers outlined that my son was to leave with me. Ok, if that's what the papers say, then that is what I will do. Knowing my legal rights I knew my son was leaving with me.

I continued to sit as time passed. She would be a full hour late. It was a hot August day in Florida, so sitting under that little tree, waiting for someone who was trying to abduct my son, I probably had good reason to become hot, bothered and angry. Yet when she arrived, what occurred was as if from a movie. They pulled up and my son ran into my arms, all excited about the new adventure his mother had sold him on. "We can Skype like we do with Grandpa!" With my son in my arms, I started to slowly move away from his mother as she was served the papers. All hell broke loose at that point. She went ballistic, screaming and yelling, trying to pull our son from my arms, yelling hate and curses. Strangely, I did not get mad; I did not yell. I had faith that this was going to be ok. Amazingly, we had the court papers, my son who I thought was gone not two hours ago was in my arms-- faith had gotten me this far; I was going to keep riding it.

I kept trying to soothe my now-hysterical son and calmly explained to my ex that this was not how things should be done. Everything was crisp and precise, ultra vivid yet somewhat surreal and dreamy--the people walking by, the flags fluttering in the breeze, white clouds against a blue sky. Everything was moving slowly. I could see the scene clearly, wondering what passersby were thinking and calmly soothing our son over and over. Our son was crying; his mother was pulling him hard by the neck, while I had a firm grip around his waist, whispering over and over in his ear that *everything would be ok. When my ex raised her fists to strike me I went to the ground, protecting our son from the blows with my body. She no longer had a grip. She continued to yell and scream, but I could keep her from grabbing hold of our son.*

Once we were free from her grip, the onslaught of verbal hate continued. Calmly, I figured the best way to get our son into the car. His car seat in the back would not do, because he would be unprotected while I was getting into the driver's seat. The front passenger seat was the best option. Maneuvering our son to the front passenger seat, through the driver's seat, I could maintain his safety and keep his mother at bay. His mother asked to be allowed to kiss our son, which I did allow, and off we went as the police were pulling up. It was then, as I was leaving the parking lot, that the process server called me, letting me know he had called the police on her when she got violent. Therefore I decided that the best course of action was to head to the lawyer's office. If I had done anything wrong, I was not going to be accused of running away. By the time we got to the lawyer's office my son had calmed.

Standing in the court two weeks later, my ex did not show up, as she had continued on to Pennsylvania. At that time the judge ordered temporary custody to me. However, he ordered that before the next time we came to him, we were to go to mediation. She did show up for the mediation. After talking to me for a few minutes the mediator went to the room where she was sitting. Two minutes later the mediator came back into the room I was in and said, "She won't mediate. She thinks she has something on you that will get the judge to award her custody." Strangely, it took a few moments before it hit me. "Oh yeah, I am an alcoholic in recovery. I have been sober for two and half years." Then I laid out my weekly recovery commitments, meetings, sponsor, sponsees and service work. "Yes, that's what she has on you and yes, that I see that is no longer an issue."

For the next 6 months while we awaited trial, knowing that she was going to go after my past active alcoholism, I documented all I did for my recovery. Rarely a day went by where I did not do something for my recovery, with most days having multiple entries. This was going to be the cornerstone of her case and we needed to show that my alcoholism was as much in the past as could be. As my sponsor continued to remind me, "Even O.J. got off." Throughout it all she tried to push buttons at every turn. Sometimes she was more successful than others, but eventually I learned to not take the bait. Regardless, it was a long six months, with an almost constant anxiety that I might lose my son. It was not easy on me or my wife, not to mention that higher powers (I mean lawyers) are expensive, but each step along the way we had faith in trying to do the right, best thing for our son.

When all was said and done, the judge deemed that my alcoholism was a thing of the past and my son was to live with my wife and me. Through it all my sponsor reminded me how none of this would have been possible if I had been drinking. This was faith in the program, faith in the fellowship in action, faith that if I kept doing the next "right thing," things would work out. At each stage of the process we worked with acceptance, that regardless of the outcome that we could accept it. If the judge had deemed it best for my son to be with my ex, then we would have accepted it, knowing that we had done everything in our power. At the beginning we made the decision that we could not just lie down and let his mother take him. We needed to know that we had done what we could, that we were trying to do what was best for him.

If I had been drinking I never would have gone to the lawyer that Monday morning. I would have let my son go and bemoaned it. I would have gone to the bar to get drunk when she said they were packed and leaving. I would have berated her verbally and burned bridges. This would have fueled a serious binge. Instead, I continued to have faith in the program. I went to meetings, shared, and called people. I believed with all my heart that drinking would not solve this problem or make it better. I allowed sobriety to be my higher power and I had faith that in the end, being sober I would be ok regardless of the outcome. All the small battles and victories of sobriety, all the victories I witnessed in the rooms led me to have faith that I did not have to drink over this. Every step of the way through the ordeal and trial was aided by the fellowship and the people in my support network.

Going to the retreat that weekend, with all the emotional energy of hearing that she wanted to take my son from me, was the perfect thing to do *just then. The result was that I also developed faith in the practice of meditation, that the practice can handle all these emotions that felt so large and powerful. I am an alcoholic and have never been good with my emotions. Sitting in the parking lot without losing my seat showed me how to continue through the energy, that it would have a beginning, middle and end. Throughout the next six months, with the constant emotional ups and downs, working practices like tonglen and metta were instrumental to keeping my heart open and preventing that "why is this happening to me" mentality. (Tonglen and metta are two traditional practices which we will discuss in greater detail further in the steps. Tonglen helps us exchange self for other, connecting us to the pain of others and all people, whereas metta helps us open our hearts to those we love (and hate) and all people.) As a result I developed a deep faith in these practices by working them in all kinds of situations. In the end I believe that maintaining an open heart to the mother of my child showed through and was a major reason why my son is with me today.*

Step Four

Made a searching and fearless moral inventory of ourselves. (Big Book of AA)

Once we have made the decision to go through the remainder of the steps, we need to "get into action." However, many will use this as an excuse to go no further. Buried in our cocoon are memories and behaviors better left hidden we think. Why would anyone want to go back and look at all of these tragedies, dramas, and failures? Yet it is vitally important to look back, to see where we have come from and to look again at these old stories with new eyes. We cannot go forward until we have a sense of where we have been.

When we lived in our cocoons, all our stories, experiences, and thoughts were seen the way our mind saw them. We were "insane." Our filter was distorted. Now we get a chance to reexamine our lives with that understanding. Chances are we will discover some new things about stories that we were once certain about. In fact most of us could only see as far as the immediate "so-and-so hurt ME" and "how can this happen to ME?" As NA's Basic Text states, "We are trying to free ourselves of living in the old, useless patterns. We take the Fourth Step to grow and gain strength and insight."

It is important to remember gentleness, because as Pema Chodron states (and I'm paraphrasing), we would not let anyone talk to a friend the way we talk to ourselves. This gentleness is extremely important to hold onto as we go forward into Step Four because we will see both the good and bad in ourselves. Some will erroneously believe that they were the worst of the worst of the worst, while others will think they hurt no one but themselves. We needed a sense of fearless and daring in our breaking from the cocoon. We will need that fearlessness, courage and discipline to hold off being judge and jury about our past and allow ourselves to work through Step Four.

In Step Two we accepted that our views of the world and ourselves were completely skewed, i.e., insane, particularly when it came to our addictions. Truth is, we had no idea how badly skewed we were, not only about our addictions but about most things. Uncovering the reality of our actions may be jarring to some, so it is important to keep that gentleness in our hearts. We need to live in this moment, just this moment, not concerning ourselves with Step Five. Just as we work with one breath at a time, one day at a time, we cannot worry about Step Five. There will be a lot happening between writing the step and reading it.

Making a Start

One of the most important aspects of this step is to do the step to the best of our abilities, without judgment. As we put our life down on paper, we will see our glaring faults and repetitive behaviors. In the same way that while we are sitting in meditation we do not judge the thought as good or bad, our goal at first is just to get that stuff down on paper. Later this step becomes a tool for examining the causes and conditions of a problem. Generally this is not a one-and-done process. As we continue through our sobriety, more will be revealed and we may wish to examine events in our lives, both in the past and in the present, using this Fourth Step inventory method.

The Lies We Tell Ourselves

Fancying myself a writer at one point of my life, I was very much looking forward to getting down to this step. I was looking forward to it because now my sponsor would really be able to understand how the world had wronged me. That was not what happened in the end.

That one period of my life where I fancied myself a writer was a drug and alcohol filled "adventure" along the Kerouac line (except we never got farther than a few states away). This was post graduating from college, where all my friends waited tables and I was "taking a break" after such a hard final year at college. That final year of college was by all normal definitions a disaster, culminating in a third trip to the emergency room two nights before graduation for (another set of) stitches in my drafting hand after putting my fist through an ex-girlfriend's French door in a drunken rage. To recuperate from that hard year of college, I reasoned I needed a break. I needed a nice, relaxing job so I could do some serious drinking. It made perfect sense to me at the time.

A job as a camp counselor seemed the right speed. Summer moved to fall and I got a job working at a bookstore. I continued to drink all night most every night, having brilliant literary discussions and adventures that I was writing into a semi-autobiographical adventure. In my version of the adventures, I was the tragic hero, gallivanting around drinking, drugging and chasing women. Eventually, knowing I could not maintain this minimum wage, drink all night lifestyle, I got a very low level job in my career field, drafting concrete shop drawings in a factory. I kept the job at the bookstore because the factory paid better but had no benefits and the bookstore had benefits. Life was a whirlwind of working two full time jobs, drinking six out of seven nights a week, getting three hours of sleep a night, going from one job to the next, to the bar, then writing and more drinking until I passed out. One day I went in to the boss at the factory job asking for a raise after coming into work half-drunk and stoned every day for the previous six months. For a raise, I was willing to come in sober and alert. He was not very thrilled with the terms of my bargain.

One Friday in March of 1996, I was driving home from the drafting job and I did not have to be at the bookstore till noon the next day. What struck me as a brilliant and vitally necessary idea was that I needed to go back to Chuck's. Chuck's was a basement bar at my alma mater, four hours away. I called Chuck's home for my entire 5 years of higher education and I needed to go back there. I would be ok if I could just get to Chuck's. All the anxiety and panic would subside if I could just get back to those cozy confines. This was the time before cell phones, so I went back to my rented room and made some phone calls. No one would come with me on a four-hour drive just to get drunk at some college, sleep on some, and wake at eight to be back by noon the next day. Oh well, I headed out anyway. I got about 45 minutes out when I realized how foolish it was to do this alone, so I turned around. When I walked back into my room the phone rang. A particular girl I was very interested in was on the other end and she agreed to the madness.

Seven months later we were married. Between that first phone call and our eloping there was the first attempt at trying to get my drinking under control. With less alcohol some of my craziness began to settle down, at least the outward craziness. One week she went away on a family vacation and without her around my drinking went off the charts. Obviously her being around was the solution. The way to have her around all the time was for us to get married. Our first years of marriage were not an easy transition for either of us. We fought often. Frequently I would snap after some minor rub or jab, storming off to go get drunk. I was still writing but was struggling to make any sense of all the emotions I was experiencing and did not want to be feeling. It wasn't long after that, with all this emotional energy building up and struggling to express it through words, that she bought me some paints and canvas.

This began the painting period, as expression and therapy. For a decade painting would be my primary form of artistic expression. My daytime was spent drafting to $\frac{1}{8}$" accuracy, so my painting was abstract with a 2" house painter's brush. After our divorce I would stay up all night long painting and drinking. The only sober nights were the nights I had our daughters with me. When their visits were over, I would drop them off at their mother's and return to my studio apartment, to get drunk and paint. I would not admit I was an alcoholic. I drank because I was shattered by the dissolution of my marriage. I drank because I did not want to feel. In reality I drank because I was an alcoholic and those were very convenient excuses that let everyone, including myself, look the other way.

Being lonely but unable to overcome my own shyness and lack of self-esteem, I turned to an Internet dating site for single parents my therapist recommended. After a few failed dates locally, I met a very beautiful woman with a daughter around the age of my daughters. We started chatting, then talking, then visiting. Our first date lasted a weekend, our second date a week. By the end of our first year dating long distance she moved up to New Jersey to be with me.

It is easy to hide being an alcoholic when you are dating long distance. That year of dating was not the easiest and maybe we both thought things would settle down once we were no longer traveling a thousand miles to see each other. Unfortunately, the gaining of a stepdaughter, the struggles with my ex-wife and my worry about my own daughters and then having a child together caused a lot of tension in our lives. As the Big Book says, "All of us felt at times we were regaining control, but such intervals, usually brief, were inevitably followed by still less control." Eventually sober days would become few and far between. I continued to paint. All the pain I felt came out in grotesque forms on canvas.

When that relationship ended I was unemployed and bankrupt on more levels than I realized. Stubborn as I was, I continued to struggle on, pretending that everything was ok and that my drinking was not a problem. At the very end of my drinking, my painting had become almost manic. Huge canvases were on every wall and open floor of my apartment. Each night I got drunk and painted till the early dawn, a manic crescendo of working on multiple pieces at a time. In the morning I would wake, discover the work I had done the night before, scrub the paint off my hands and drag myself into the work.

Basic Sobriety

It Was All Bravado

In other words I felt like a pretty expressive person, or at least I portrayed myself as an expressive person because the reality was that all of this was sleight of hand. This was not expressing my true emotions and feelings; this was veiled innuendo to show I was a sensitive, troubled soul, but I was not letting you anywhere near getting to know the real person inside. Therapists and doctors heard bits and pieces, enough to deem me not crazy or enough to prescribe pills, but never the whole picture. All the expressiveness was a lie I hid behind so that no one would probe any deeper. All the anger and rage blustered to wall up this person you would probably think dull and unworthy of even friendship let alone love. I was not letting you see that person.

Three Column Inventory

When I started to write the inventory, my sponsor had me use three columns: fears, resentments, and what I felt bad about (i.e., sins and transgressions). Begin with the fears to help get the ink flowing: fears of snakes and heights opened the way for some deeper fears to find the light of day. Fear, in one form or another, was the root of most of my behaviors. "Driven by a hundred forms of fear, self-delusion, self-seeking and self-pity, we step on the toes..." (Big book of AA). Many of these fears were rational and sane, many of them were irrational and petty. How many of our actions occur to protect ourselves from these fears, being experienced or exposed?

When we list our fears we see all the little soft spots that we try to protect. Many of our resentments grew out of protecting these tender and sensitive spots. The resentment list was the spot I was going to show my sponsor--how I had been wronged. I had been wronged by my parents, my family, my wives, and bosses. I was going to lay it all out.

Funny thing is that it didn't quite go the way I imagined. Why? Causes and conditions. As an example, I was angry at my first wife for wanting a divorce. But why would she want a divorce? There, once I stopped pointing the finger at her, I started to see her wanting a divorce was the direct result of years of my selfish and self-centered behavior, of fights I instigated and an increasing amount of drinking. No one comes to the word divorce on a whim. You get there because for years your husband acted like a petulant child, raging off to get drunk, then coming home begging for forgiveness. You say that because you have been unhappy for a long, long time and your husband only thought of his own needs and desires. Causes and conditions resulted in the divorce. I was always frightened of losing her, of her discovering who I really was. What would happen if I was not cooler than that guy at the next table? A better lover? Smarter? Someone would take her away, right? I would be without this woman I was insanely in love with. How could she love me if I was constantly trying to be something I was not? For the first time in my life I was seeing and admitting that I had a major part to play in these causes and conditions. Having written out the list of fears first, separate from any situation or person, I could then see them underlying all the actions that caused the resentments.

Before the act of listing my resentments I never realized the extent to which the events of the past occupied my mind in the present. I was amazed at how often I would be driving along, suddenly noticing myself fuming about some person or situation from years ago. Catching myself in the resentment, I would write that person down. The funny thing wasn't the realization of how much of my time was spent rehashing these minor, or major, events, but how when I would get home and go to add that person to the list, I would find that I had already listed them a half dozen times before. It got so bad that I needed to use an Excel spreadsheet (yes, I am that kind of geek) to keep track of all of this and to keep myself from listing things over and over again.

The next column was sins and transgressions, or basically what I felt really bad about. Some people believe this third column should be the sex list but my sponsor did not. I still have yet to see what purpose beyond shame and guilt a list of all the people one has slept with illuminates. The major women in my life were all covered in my resentment list and once I got honest with "my part in it" all the patterns and stuff I was hiding about those relationships came out. There were the minor and middle women, but it was easy to see the patterns of my behaviors in all those relationships without trying to remember each of them. If I felt guilty about a particular something it was going to show up and if I had left it just to women I had slept with, some of the worst guilt would never have found its way to paper.

Two More Columns?

The 12x12 reminds us that we need to list our assets as well as our liabilities. Maybe we can use another column or two, a "Good Qualities" and a "Good things I've done" column. This way we do not morbidly tilt the scale and throw ourselves into a tizzy before we even get to the end of the step. We must avoid the quagmire that can be created by the "Oh look what a piece of dirt I am and here is the list to prove it" mentality. Even though we may have done a number of regrettable actions, there were probably a number of good ones sprinkled through our lives. With the penchant of the human memory to focus on the negative, it is important to remember the positive elements and moments of our lives.

I believe that here, the goal is to find the middle ground, the middle way. As alcoholics and addicts we typically are "egomaniacs with inferiority complexes." So we are either the worst or the best and what we really need is an honest look at ourselves. We need to develop a proper attitude about our past actions. Sakyong Mipham says that we need to have appropriate levels of embarrassment and shame. If we do not feel even the slightest embarrassment, it is because our egos have grown to feel that we can do no wrong. Now, shame here is used not as a heavy-handed label of condemnation.

Shame is an indicator of non-virtuous behavior, as actions below our own personal code of conduct. When we are acting in this way we are acting as the center of our own universe and have little regard for others. Our ego has grown too big. We need an appropriate amount of embarrassment and shame to help us see where we have erred and where we can direct our behavior going forward.

Morality and Sin

The AA program of recovery places a great emphasis on housecleaning and inventory-taking. Bill notes that people throughout the ages have used self inventory to great success. He also gives a pretty good piece of litmus to test against: where have we been driven by "fear, self-delusion, self-seeking and self-pity" (p. 62) and again further on, "Where had we been selfish, dishonest, self-seeking and frightened?" (p. 67). If we just used these categories to judge our behavior against we would have a thorough inventory of our negative actions.

Within the non-theistic traditions there is not the same emphasis on "sin" as it was understood by the early AAers. In the Judeo-Christian belief system to sin meant to perform "an immoral act considered to be a transgression against divine law." Generally the result was an eternity of suffering in hell. Instead, if we removed the whole divine law part and just looked at sin to mean "that which caused suffering," in the theistic tradition you have a choice between good and bad, right and wrong, heaven and hell. In the Buddhist tradition it would probably be better to use the words "skillful and unskillful" to describe our thoughts, speech and actions in any given moment. Or we may use virtue and non-virtue.

When we look at concepts like good and bad, they are generally just labels we place on a situation. Oh, isn't it bad that you got a cold? Oh, isn't it good that you got a raise? You never really can know the answer to those statements. At best, in the moment, we have a maybe. Remember, we are not trying to abide by some arbitrary set of rules created by some external mythical being that will result in a final score of pass and fail. As humans we will make our choices and they will fall somewhere on the spectrum between skillful and unskillful or virtuous and unvirtuous. Usually our intentions and actions will not be so black and white. They will be a mixture of good and bad, somewhat akin to the "Director" in the Big Book who is "really a self-seeker even when trying to be kind."

In the Judeo-Christian world of "Original Sin" so much emphasis is placed on the negative aspect of our actions. Right from birth you are bad, so you are trying to make up for that negative by doing extra positive. Much of our lives are governed by rules and laws, all meant to "protect" us. However, they are almost always written in the "don't do this, don't do that" mentality. For example "Thou shalt not kill" seems pretty straightforward. Killing is bad and you go to hell for doing it. What about the flip side, Thou shall respect life? Further, there are gradations of killing in our society today. Kill a man and that's bad, kill a deer and that's good. Kill a bad man and that is good, kill a good deer and that is bad. What seemed pretty straightforward can become quite convoluted. We a) aim for the virtuous and skillful, even if we fall short we do so in a positive way or b) don't live up to the strictest level of virtuous and skillful actions we endeavor to minimize our negative behaviors.

Even the most virtuous action may have non-virtuous motives and as you may see in the rooms, even the worst actions can teach valuable lessons to ourselves and others.

Ten Acts

Trungpa states, "Since we experience freakiness and unwholesomeness continuously in our ordinary life, we may begin to feel that we are being cheated. If we are theists, we get angry at God, thinking that God has cheated us; if we are non-theists, we blame karma. In either case, we feel we have been cheated by somebody, somewhere. We begin to be resentful and doubtful, and we find that sitting on our meditation cushion is painful." (Unknown source)

How did we end up experiencing the karma we have to deal with? What might the "rules" be to help guide us going forward? If we are going to blame karma for our current state of freakiness, or rather unmanageable life, we need to take a moment to look at the factors that go into that karma. The freakiness comes from our fundamental aggression with ourselves and the world. Fundamental aggression is not a polite form of aggression but based on a deeper level of anger and resentment. If we are to rid ourselves of this aggression we need to examine the causes and conditions as they relate to karma. Therefore a good moral barometer for the Fourth Step could be the Ten Acts of Unmeritorious and Meritorious Karma. The Ten Acts of Unmeritorious Karma are: taking life, stealing, sexual misconduct, telling lies, causing intrigue, negative words, gossip, envy, hoping to do harm and disbelieving in the truth. The Meritorious Acts are the flip side of the Unmeritorious acts.

When we are filled with aggression and we come upon someone, we either want to kill them, steal from them or have sex with them. We are looking at what we can get from the situation. What is also of interest to note is how much of the list is based on our speech. There is so much harm that we can cause with our words. We use our words and our silences as strongly as we use our body.

When we use speech in unmeritorious ways we do so to promote or protect ourselves. In active addiction we lied to cover our addiction: we lied to ourselves; we lied to protect our own security. We told people what we thought would get us in the least amount of trouble. Trying to divide people by making some of them friends and others the enemy is causing intrigue. We drew some people in and pushed others out in an almost constant push-and-pull drama of relationships. When we could not control people with our lies and intrigue we moved to negative words. We sought to destroy with these words; we sought to destroy the pride and egos that kept them apart from and above us. Those whom we could not destroy directly with negative words; we attempted to destroy covertly with gossip. We created chatter that would pull down those we could not entice, deceive or destroy. We hated them for being better than us in some way, so we sought to bring them down to our level. Can you find these actions in your dealings with those on your resentment list?

What we wanted to destroy with gossip was created by envy. In our mind we felt inferior to others and that caused terrible pains for us. We were jealous and envious of others, because we felt we were never going to be enough. Nothing would ever be enough on almost every level. We had an acute sense of poverty mentality. Our jealousy and envy would lead us to deeper thoughts of hoping harm and bad things happened to others. These two acts, of jealousy and envy, are the seeds of resentment. Even those whom we loved and cared for we often were envious of and resented them for it. All of this led us to disbelieve the truth. We would never accept the truth because it shone the light on our unmeritorious actions. Taking that further, when presented with anything of virtue or sacredness we disbelieved the truth, looking for lies, loopholes and reasons to point a sanctimonious finger. Our own wretchedness would not allow that truth to exist. Surely if we were doing these things, we surmised that everyone else had to be doing them as well.

All these actions furthered the fruition of negative karma.

In essence all the positive versions of the unmeritorious acts are the ten meritorious actions. These acts produce virtue and positive karmic results. We respect life, practice generosity, develop friendships and observe sexual appropriateness. With our speech we practice telling the truth, being straightforward and using kind words and simple speech. In our minds we develop openness instead of envy, gentleness instead of doing harm and understanding sacredness. These are the positive behaviors we hear described in the rooms of recovery.

In regard to doing the fourth step we can remember the times where we practiced some of these virtues. We can note times of generosity and kindness. When we focus so precisely on our negative aspects we forget that we had positive aspects as well. We can use both sides of the acts of merit to do our inventory by.

Discipline Brings Joy

When we leave the cocoon behind, we enter the realm of the Snow Lion. The Snow Lion is said to frolic in the highland mountains, enjoying the freshness of the situation, the freedom from the cocoon. The Snow Lion is energetic and vibrant. We feel this energy in our life now. The Snow Lion leaps from mountain to mountain, for a moment completely free in the highland air before returning to the earth. This is our recovery, moments of freedom, and then we return to earth. The Lion is joyful because it has discipline.

Trungpa defined discipline as "that which cools off neurotic heat." It cools off our neurotic heat because we are more pragmatic, precise and realistic. For the most part, alcoholics and addicts tend to shy away from discipline, at least discipline as defined by Merriam Webster: "control that is gained by requiring that rules or orders be obeyed and punishing bad behavior." Here we are looking at a different type of discipline, because it is imposed by no one but ourselves. We continue to sit. We continue to go to meetings. We begin to notice that something is changing. That neurotic heat that burned so fiercely within us has indeed started to cool down.

Discipline of Commitments

Not having a clue about Twelve Step meetings before I found myself in one, I was lost when it came to the discipline of going to meetings, calling my sponsor, and all the other bits that helped keep people sober. When I went to my first meeting I was shaking and lost. Some guy came up to me after the meeting and gave me his phone number and a big book. I called him the next night because I was in intense pain with the desire to drink. That phone call miraculously got me through to the next day. I did not go to a meeting that day but I did not drink. It was painful and a struggle to get through the day sober. I didn't quite understand how it all worked yet.

Basic Sobriety

A few more painful days passed and I found there was a clubhouse near my office. Seeking some relief from the emotional and physical stress of new sobriety, I went there on lunch break. A few minutes after I sat down, another guy walked in, shaking hands, fist pumps and high fives with everyone he passed till he took a seat next to me. This group started off the meeting by having everyone say their name and sobriety date if they so choose. Around the room I heard people say everything from a few days, like me, to decades, which was mind-blowing. After the meeting the guy who sat next to me, put his arm around my shoulder, asked me a few questions and told me to call him that night. I do not know exactly why I called him that night. I called him because he said he wanted to know how I was doing. This was how I found my sponsor, or I really should say that my sponsor found me. He would turn out to be exactly who I needed as a sponsor. I just did not know it at the time.

I continued to struggle, going to a meeting here and there. I had no discipline when it came to meetings. From day one my sponsor insisted on one act of discipline: to call him every day to let him know how my day went. For some reason I did, frequently calling him at 2am when my day was ending, so that I could just leave a message without actually having to talk to him much. Yet for some reason, just having that little bit of accountability, I was getting through each day. Frequently I would panic, or have the desire to drink, and I would call him during the day and he would talk me off the ledge. It was only after a little bit of time that I realized that I seemed saner on days I went to meetings. Being the good alcoholic and not wanting to do things that were good for me, I experimented with it. What happened if I went to a meeting? What if I didn't go? This went on for a few weeks--a process of staying sober but only dipping my toes into AA.

It wasn't till well past my first 90 days that I started to do the "suggested" 90 meetings in 90 days. What happened then was what happens to most people who undertake the discipline of a meeting a day. In the beginning it's a bit of a drudgery as the days tick by. Then something happens where you start to enjoy the meetings. Maybe it's not that you actually enjoy the meetings but you enjoy the result, the serenity or momentary peace of mind. As time went on, keeping myself closer to the program, my network grew, as I was now a regular at certain meetings, and those creeping thoughts of drinking started to become fewer. Soon I began looking forward to my daily meeting. When things got tense, I would even go to more than one meeting a day. In the end, the 90 days came and went and I kept going with it. Why stop doing something that was working? Sometime after the 10th or 11th 90 in a row, my sponsor and I agreed that I could ease up on my meeting schedule.

The home group my sponsor introduced me to, after months of my resisting, was a commitment meeting. Members made certain commitments to their sponsors and then reported back on them to the group. These commitments were things like going to meetings, calling your sponsor, meeting face to face with your sponsor and meeting with sponsees if you had them. You didn't need to think anymore about how many meetings you needed to go to in a week or if you needed to call your sponsor today. This was a method of imposing discipline on an undisciplined lot, with a very good success rate. The daily phone call was the beginning of a structure to my sobriety. This discipline laid the groundwork for further development. In fact, without the groundwork of discipline there is only so far we will get, only so far the results will take you.

Discipline of Meditation

In Shambhala one of the fundamental disciplines is the act of meditation. The Kagyu and Nyingma traditions that Trungpa was a lineage holder for are practice lineages. It is taught that nothing could progress without the practice of meditation. When you sat down you touched the earth, you sat solidly on the earth while your head touched the heavens. You connect the two. When we are sitting we connect heaven and earth; we also connect our mind and our body. We will not know how to do this if we do not practice meditation. Learning to connect mind and body is an important step in the development of the warrior. It is also important for the sense of wellness and confidence we need for a strong sobriety.

So the first act is the discipline to sit. Then we can connect our mind and body, or heaven and earth. When our mind and body are aligned we are present with the world and we flow effortlessly through it. We are not wondering if we should just move this way or that way; we see the big picture and are able to work with the world. When our mind and body are not connected we cannot even pour a simple cup of tea. We will be clumsy because our body is not in sync with our mind, or we will be distracted and pour the tea on our foot. It is at that moment we get feedback from the world that our mind and body are not connected. The practice of sitting meditation is where we tend the soil of our minds so that we can plant the seeds of virtue and compassion. It is through the practice of sitting meditation that we develop gentleness and goodness.

When you sit, you can play games with yourself and avoid what arises or you can honestly be there and experience and let go of what arises. As your thoughts arise, you practice letting them go. When you sit all your habitual patterns of avoidance and entertainment will come up to greet you. It is by noticing and letting go of the habitual patterns that you can begin to see your own style of avoidance. When you sit, you not only work with your mind but you work with your body. You sit in a manner that is uplifted and regal. Your strong back and open heart manifest from the sitting position. Simply by sitting and returning to your body, you begin to change your habit of living purely in your head. You start to align your body and mind, your experience and intellect. When that happens there are moments, or gaps of being on the spot. You drift off and catch yourself in another daydream and then you pull yourself back and for a moment you are awake and present. Our mind and body are aligned and that taps into a natural, self-existing fountain of energy within you.

Fearlessness

Learning to hold our seats when we are overtaken by emotion and thought is important. As we continue to examine our past and our fearless moral inventory, we will be faced with a number of things we do not like about ourselves. We drank many a drink to avoid having to look at that part of us and say, "Yes, I did that." We learn while sitting not to judge our thoughts; whether it is a good thought or bad thought, we just let it go. Not only will we encounter the memories of those not so memorable moments, but also our habitual pattern of talking to ourselves about those moments. We will find that we beat ourselves up a lot for those past actions. We get caught up in the story and there we are again and again. All of it will come up when we sit, so we need discipline to stay in our seat, to hold the spot and return to the breath.

This is much of what the 4th Step is all about: something comes up; we write it down and move on to the next item. Sometimes we sit with the thought a little. We apply some of our inquisitiveness to the feeling or thought. *Why do I feel this way about so and so? Why did I say those mean things to that person?* Most importantly, we do not judge what we discover about ourselves. This is the beginning of fearlessness. We see all our fears and we begin to get acquainted with them. We lean into them. We poke at them and instead of biting back at us, they pop. No matter which format you use, which set of guidelines you hold yourself to, give yourself the space that your sitting practice has given you. Just get it down on paper, and when you get too caught up in the past or start to worry about having to tell this to someone, you just bring yourself back to this moment and see in this moment you are just writing words on paper.

Most of us expect that when we first sit down to meditate that we will find this perfect place of serenity and peace. What really happens is that we can barely sit still for five minutes, let alone stay with our breath or find some peace. Usually, people say to me that they just can't stop thinking long enough to meditate and that they wish they could do it. I can only speak for my meditative experiences but I believe they relate here to the fourth step. When we first look at the fourth step many people freak out because of what they think they will have to reveal about themselves. Comparing that to the process of sitting down to meditate, all that stuff that we have been stuffing down and avoiding for years bubbles to the surface. At first it feels the exact opposite of what we thought that meditation was to be about. The experience is anything but soothing. This is where the discipline is so important. There are some traditional obstacles to meditation, but this obstacle of "that was not what I expected" is more like a pre-obstacle. We won't even get to those obstacles if we can't get beyond the reality of meditation compared to our expectation. This is the bravery of the warrior and it takes all of our discipline to stay on the cushion some days. Some days we will hold our seat, and some days we won't, but we need the gentleness and discipline to try again each day, fresh and new. Everyone thinks they are doing something wrong at first, that the person next to them is meditating so much better than they are. We have some experience with hope and faith, so we feel that continuing to sit is a worthwhile practice. This is not just intellectual mumbo jumbo; we have some practical experience of sitting. So we stay with it.

In the Shambhala tradition, for the most part, we meditate with our eyes open with a soft, slightly unfocused gaze. We are not trying to drift off into some mystical place but rather we are trying to learn to be present with whatever arises. Initially I thought that that meant whatever arose to the visual sense perceptions, that if Buddha appeared to me or aliens dropped out of the sky, I needed to be ready. Sadly, that was not why we sit with our eyes open. We cannot turn off our skin or our ears, so we do not turn off our eyes either. Open eyes help us remain grounded when we drift off into those fantasies or rehashes. With our eyes open we are connected to the space around us. At first when a strong emotion or memory arises, it feels like a raging bull in a tight pen. Everything seems claustrophobic and the energy is intense. Sitting with the emotion, connected to space, allows our minds to open, to loosen up around the emotion. We let it go into that space and now the raging bull has a wide field to roam in. Soon the energy of the bull fades because it has so much space.

This is what sitting promises us, that space, but at first it will feel the exact opposite. We think there must be an easier, softer way, but there isn't. We need to sit to struggle through the beginning to find that ultimately what seemed like the difficult route is really the easier, softer way. At each step we wish there was an easier, softer way, or a half measure that will get us by. There isn't. We need to give our honest effort through it all. That may mean struggling through what seems like an eternity waiting for the gong to ring, or it may mean struggling with that blank piece of paper.

More Will Be Revealed

You will not write the perfect 4th step. We do the best we can at that moment in time. Each of us will sit down with a variety of emotions about the step itself. If we are honest in our endeavor, disciplined enough to finish it, we will have all manner of information to work with. The honest effort part is important. I have seen people put up a good front on the fourth step list, afraid to tell some of their deeper secrets. "We are only as sick as our secrets" and those who have held back on their fourth step inevitably drank again. This list will hold the seeds for the next steps, so it is important to be as thorough as possible. More will be revealed, so we can always add to it, whether formally or in minor ways in the future.

For me even months after getting through the Steps, there were moments when major layers of fog seemed to lift, revealing a fresh batch of memories. There was also a wall in the fog that I could sense but not see. I knew it was there both from a meditation and sobriety standpoint--there was something I was not ready to see yet. When I was ready I knew the wall would fall and so I continued to sit and work the program. Eventually that wall did fall, revealing a core series of causes and conditions for why I behaved the way I did throughout so much of my life.

Regardless of where we are, we must not procrastinate finishing this step. We should not sit on this information for too long before we complete the process with the Fifth Step. Having pulled up a great deal of fears, resentments and the stuff that gnawed at us in the night, we are raw and vulnerable. We have taken the first step in processing this information. Right now it is just data, lists of our "neurotic heat" and habitual patterns. We need to move to further understanding of all this data with the Fifth Step.

Step Five

Admitted to God, to ourselves, and to another human being the exact nature of our wrongs. (Big Book of AA)

There is something to the power of honest confession that most of us missed going through life. We told our tales of woe to gain sympathy or forgiveness. We were like magicians telling the audience to look over here to our right hand so they would not see what was in our left hand. We were very happy to look at the faults of others, so that our faults would seem justified or trivial. We rarely let anyone know our true selves because we are ashamed of whom that true self may be. As a result we build a wall (or cocoon), a line where you can know this about me, but not that. There is a definite distinction between self and other. When we accomplish Step Five that line between self and other, between you and everyone else, begins to fade.

So with our Fourth Step in hand we take further action. The written word I can take and put on a shelf, never to acknowledge again. This is what we tried to do with our using and abusing; we kept searching for a way to forget that knowledge about ourselves. It would never stay hidden on the shelf, or we were constantly terrified that someone would discover it. Writing it down and putting it on a shelf would not be enough to move ourselves out of our addictive patterns. We need to do something different with this information this time around. Instead of pushing it away, we actually have to dive further into it. We need to take possession of our deeds. But how?

God, Ourselves and Another Human Being

It is through our connection to other human beings that a good human society can grow, a society based on kindness and virtue. The concept of an Enlightened Society begins here, through one–on–one communication. This is where it all begins, an act of open communication between two people. When two people communicate from a position of goodness, to help one another, the foundation of good society is laid.

We connect, one-on-one, with another human being. Without our armor, without our cocoons, we bring all the worst stuff to the table--all the stuff that we thought only we had done; only someone like me could do or fear, and they smile and nod. In fact, they did it too! They felt the way we felt, responded in the same manner and in the end reached the same conclusion that we did. Suddenly we are not alone in the world. We can connect to another human being directly and purely. When we do this we are not shunned or ridiculed but accepted and loved. The connection begins with one person and grows to the fellowship. We begin to have genuine relationships with others and the world. We are just like everyone else, just moving along day by day, no better and no worse (for the most part) than everyone else.

The threefold act of "God, ourselves and another human being" transforms our past actions. Our past actions begin on the page as intellectual fodder. Through the process of saying our list three times, we slowly and incrementally bring the list into our heart and experience. The first time is to God or a higher power, who is in essence something outside of ourselves. Admitting to God only got us so far before. Maybe we had some luck white-knuckling sobriety or abstinence in the past, but we would always fall back into our old ways. *God understands; he knows me better than I know myself, so why bother with him?* we may have reasoned. The pledges we made to ourselves or him, even to loved ones and judges, are easy to disregard when they are just in our head.

The second time we say it, instead of cowering from our past we can begin to connect with it, to own it. We move deeper now by telling it to ourselves. We can look at our list and read it out loud to ourselves; with gentleness and openness we see the fears, resentments, and confusions of our past and the way our passion, aggression and ignorance was involved in every twist and turn of our journey. The deeds of our past begin to go from the head to the heart. *Yes, this is what I have done.* It is hard to look at this without the judgement and shame that we are accustomed to belittling ourselves with. We addicts and abusers are notorious for turning mountains into molehills and molehills into mountains. Outwardly we wanted everyone to believe we were more than the story we told ourselves about who we thought we were. Yet when we have a sense of equanimity about what we have done, we can see how many of these things were neither good nor bad. We tell ourselves that these things were better off hidden away, but now we want to bring them closer to our hearts.

This is all fine and good, but the thing that scares most of us is having to tell it to another human being. It is the discipline to face this fear that will bear the fruits of joy. The Big Book states that we can tell anyone. We can tell a doctor or therapist or, as I've heard one man do, offer a bum $20 at a bus stop and tell him your fifth step. While that may meet the technical requirements of the step, I think the results will not bear full fruition. We need to tell someone who understands, not in concept but in actuality, not intellectually but experientially. Yep, childbirth looks painful and I can have sympathy for all women who have gone through it; I just can't know what it feels like. We need to take our worst stuff to someone who has a history similar to our own, preferably addict to addict, drunk to drunk, etc. For many of us it will be the first time in our life when we will look at the person in front of us as they nod their head in agreement. Yes, they know it too. Not only have they been through it, having had similar worries, problems and fears, but they are sober or clean themselves.

When I read my Fourth Step to my sponsor one hot summer morning, we met over by the bay, a secluded spot in a park. We began easy: "I am terrified of snakes," and off it went. When we were done and a little bit sunburned a few hours later, there were no fireworks, no rocket to the 4th dimension, but something was different. What I did get when I went to sit on my porch after we were done was that fresh air. I was no longer as burdened by my past. I noticed I was sitting a little straighter, a little more comfortable in my own skin.

Immeasurables

Going from self-centered and self-serving to carrying the message to others is a long process. However, it is typical that after the completion of Step Five we no longer feel so alone in the world. We feel a part of it. Through sharing our inventory we are beginning the process of connection to the world. One way to help us cultivate our sense of connection to the world is through the practice of the Brahmaviharas, the Four Immeasurables or Limitless Ones. The Four Immeasurables are Love, Compassion, Joy and Equanimity. We need to get away from our self-centered mindset to prepare for connecting with the world around us and ultimately to help others. In our pasts we were wonderful at pretending to care for others to manipulate and get what we wanted, as we so lovingly discovered in the Fourth Step. These qualities of Love, Compassion, Joy and Equanimity are not foreign concepts. We all have these qualities within us. Many people rush out with the best intentions but without skillful means to help, and make a mess of it all. This is part of the reason why at this stage of our sobriety we have not made any direct amends and we are cautioned about trying to save others at this point. We feel great and we are full of zeal for life and the program but we still have a ways to go before we are truly ready to be of service to others.

We can take that joy we have gotten from our discipline and sobriety and jump into this practice of contemplating one or more of the immeasurable qualities. These four qualities of Love, Compassion, Joy and Equanimity are innate human qualities. As we develop further on the path our relationship with these four qualities will continue to grow and evolve. There is a formal practice known as "metta" helps us to dissolve that barrier between ourselves and others by extending our intentions first to ourselves, then to someone we love, then someone we feel neutral toward, and finally to someone we dislike or who is causing us grief. This is akin to what is said in the rooms of recovery: to pray for someone when you are angry at them. After we have sat with all those people we extend our intention to all beings in ever-growing circles. Through each step of the practice we sit with each person and each immeasurable and we begin to feel the connection between all of these people: those we love, those we couldn't care less about and those we hate. That progression is bookended by singular self and all others. Those people we feel passion, aggression and ignorance toward are the bridge to get us from self to others. Those people are all over our fourth and fifth steps.

What are we wishing these people whom we love, hate and ignore? The first Immeasurable is love or loving kindness. We wish that "all beings enjoy happiness and the root of happiness." This is not passionate love, but more a sense of goodness, brotherhood and harmony. There is a sense of connecting with each person through each one's desires to be happy. To some degree we all want love and we all need love. Yet we are not just wishing everyone to have everything they could possibly desire because that is not the root of happiness. As we go deeper into this we will discover a sense of loving kindness toward ourselves and then we can begin to extend that gentleness to others.

Compassion here is not so much sympathy for another's problems, but freeing them from suffering and not adding to that suffering ourselves. We are working with relieving the suffering of ourselves and others. From this a sense of nobility and dignity grows as we begin to do things for others for the right reasons. Compassion for others comes from developing our sense that we do not need anything, that we can actually extend ourselves.

Joy is a celebration of life. We appreciate who we are, what we have and where we are. We don't struggle with the situation but enjoy what is there. When we do this, we begin to find humor in situations. We do that because we begin to see things more clearly.

Basic Sobriety

The universe is not out to get us and some days you really do have to stub your toe 8 times before you get the message to be less caught up in your own anger. The universe is playing with you, so enjoy the dance.

Equanimity is letting go. First we let go of the outcomes. When we let go of the results we can have composure and evenness of temper. We do the work but are not attached to the results. Does that sound familiar? You hear it all the time in the rooms--that you do the work and let God handle the results. What we are letting go of is the "I want" that we used to run our lives by. I want to do what I want to do and if we aren't going to do that, I am sure going to make everyone miserable. As we continue to grow this sense of letting go on the outcomes and the situations manifests in glimpses of egolessness.

We begin at selfishness and end at egolessness. Remember, this is a process and a practice. We are going to move forward and backward, with different results each day, but one will lead to the next in the world around us. As our love grows, so will our compassion, joy and equanimity. I cannot remember exactly who said it, but they said that if we worked on perfecting one of the immeasurables we would perfect them all. As one grows so do the others. Initially we will find it extremely difficult to wish happiness on the people who rub us the wrong way. It has been my experience and I've heard that the person that people have the hardest time praying for or wishing good things for is themselves. At 42 I find myself continually learning to extend that love for myself both as who I am now and who I was in all those items on my fourth step. Little by little we can make progress toward opening our heart to ourselves and all beings. All of these limitless qualities are designed to slowly warm and thaw out the icy fortress of ego, so we no longer fight ourselves. The result is that our hearts can remain open even in the hardest of times.

It all begins with working on ourselves first and then we can move that outward. Each step outward is a little harder initially.

Sending happiness to our spouse or child is easy; moving to that guy down the street--sure why shouldn't he be happy, but our old boss--he doesn't deserve it. Therefore we apply our discipline and little by little wear away years of hatred. Suddenly we see that they were not completely to blame. We also see that if the person we told these deep dark things to experienced very similar feelings and actions, then maybe so might those we harbored such dislike for. If I fear being seen as incapable, and my sponsor fears being seen as incapable, then so might that boss who I thought doesn't deserve happiness. That thawing of the ego begins to spread toward those images of people we froze in time. Touching that basic goodness inside ourselves allows us to see it others. Just as we typically spotted all the negative qualities in others in the past, because we had them as well, now we begin to see that same goodness inside yourself in others.

The greater our compassion for others the further we will be from self-centeredness. Through the practice of the Four Immeasurables and the Fifth Step we can start to thaw decades of anger and resentment.

The Snow Lion

The proclamation of our fifth step is the Lion's Roar. The lion's roar is a fearless proclamation of the truth. We proclaim the truth of our lives, our history, the good and the bad, without judgement. The lion proclaims that all of this--from the smallest thoughts to the strongest, most powerful emotions, it is all workable. Laying out our deeds to an understanding individual, we begin to see that all these elements of our past can be related to properly. When we relate to them properly we see that they are workable. Seeing our past actions and the state of our mind through those actions we can confidently proclaim, "No!" This No is the statement that we are not going to go back to that life, to thinking that way or acting in those manners.

Basic Sobriety

Once we have proclaimed our past behaviors, a new sense of integrity, confidence and a feeling of delight begins to grow. The Snow Lion is said to leap from mountaintop to mountaintop. When we leap we leave the earth below. The earth represents those actions of our past that were less than skillful. We leave them below. We get them out, we share them, we are free and lighter. Our joy, the result of our discipline, lets us leap through the air, and we begin to let go of doubts and fears. We have laid out our true selves to someone else and that is now the beginning of a great discipline, to be ourselves. As we leap through the air the Snow Lion begins to experience the higher realms. Through our discipline, joy and integrity we begin the practice of the enlightened warrior.

According to Buddhist cosmology the realms are the six main types of existence that beings can be born into. The lower realms are the hell realm, the hungry ghost and the animal realm. The higher realms are the human, the jealous gods and the god realms. Each of these realms relates to our mental states and can be perceived as either individual lives or aspects of this lifetime. We all can relate to how through the course of a single day we can go from high to low and anywhere between. In sobriety and working the steps, these swings will become less frequent and they will not last as long. Typically we all have a particular style of dealing with the world, a view that keeps us primarily trapped in one of these realms.

Anger and aggression characterize the hell realm. It is an aggression that is so pervasive that there is no space. The anger feels like you are trying to eat yourself from the inside out. We constantly emit flames and radiate anger that continually comes back at us, perpetuating the cycle. Those periods in your life, where anger seemed to beget more anger, "We stepped on the toes of others and they retaliated." Each step escalates the game: we seethe with anger, we breathe anger and the world feeds us anger back.

Hungry ghosts have giant distended bellies and extremely small mouths and throats. Swallowing causes immense pain. This is the realm where most of us who now frequent Twelve Step meetings spent most of our time. This is the land of wanting more, or as my sponsor always reminds me, "one sounds great but 100 will not be enough." The more we have, the less we are able to be satisfied. Even while we were filling our desire we were looking ahead to the next one before we were even done with the one in front of us. Sadly, this realm has another more subtle nature than the gross desires of our addictions. Poverty mentality describes the feeling that we need to consume, that we will never be enough or have enough, in every aspect of our lives. One more iPhone, another car, job, trip, spouse, child, kiss, love letter, book, music, experience, ad infinitum. If we could just have it we would be ok, but we can never be satisfied and so we consume the people around us, taking everything we can from them. In the end we are hungry and alone.

Stubborn, ignorant and blind to our actions characterize the animal realm. Running on instinct with a simple straightforward mentality, we continue forward. We see a goal and we go toward it regardless of circumstance, without joy or humor. Our actions are direct, simple and self-justified. We trudge through life, like a pig eating whatever is in front of us, regardless of quality or substance, chomp-chomp-chomp. We justified our behavior, ignorant of the damage and chaos we were creating around us. Our delusional world was our world and we were determined to maintain that world regardless of its validity and when our world was threatened or questioned we acted with ferociousness, in self-justified anger and rage to maintain our world. When we tried to achieve the goal of joy, a nice day or a trip, our stupid animal rigidity and behavior made those moments joyless and painful.

Man stands between heaven and hell. The human realm spans qualities of the realms below in slightly more sophisticated manners and the realms above with slightly more sophomoric methods. In the human realm we are very passionate about ourselves. We are aware of ourselves and want very much to achieve happiness. That happiness always seems out of reach and separate from us, but we desire it and yet desire is too base so we dress it up, idolize it, and try to achieve some high ideal or philosophy. We use all of these methods to create our "Me-ness". We collect an endless array of knowledge and experiences to further build ourselves up. We desire to be the best and want to have the best of everything around us. Yet all those beliefs, ideals and styles are just that--our style--and we know it is not solid, such that we only want things that fit that style around us. The long-haired hippy and the Wall Street broker are both equally offended and threatened by the other. We gather those of our ilk around us and keep those threatening forces at bay. Our mind constantly struggles to balance it all, to gather and collect to keep the charade going. Mentally we are always racing, trying to get ahead, to maintain, and not to fall apart. Our mind prattles on endlessly and for all of it we in turn suffer.

The jealous god realm is filled with paranoia. Everything is the enemy. Friends are enemies and so are your enemies. Everyone is out to get something from you or past you. You are constantly on guard and protecting all your borders. Life is a constant state of comparison between yourself and others. Therefore we are jealous of those we deem "above" us and paranoid of those beneath us. Regardless of your circumstances, you regard every act as a threat and do not deal with anyone directly. You feel incredibly smart and agile, seeing all the angles and protecting yourself on all sides. Yet you are incredibly stupid because your actions are ill-conceived and unplanned. You attack what is directly before you and cannot see the bigger picture. This is aggression without anger, or so we deem it. We feel righteous and yet always below the person above us. Nothing can get past our defenses, no new idea or thoughts; these are surely attacks on our positions and therefore we must keep the enemy at bay at all costs. It is a constant battle of comparing our insides with everyone else's outsides.

God realm! We have made it to the god realm. We have worked and accumulated enough merit to get to the heaven of our desires. To work so hard is driven by a sense of hope and a sense of fear. In the end we think "I" have made it. This is still a subtle ego trip, to affirm that the we have achieved this wonderful realm. As we begin to lose that sense of hope and fear, we lose our self and that ultimately terrifies us as the "I" that has worked so hard to get there struggles to hold on. Then the sudden realization that this will not last forever dawns. We struggle to maintain it, but we must come off our high; we must run out of booze or drugs or people to sleep with. Nothing can be maintained and the result is we become terrified and angry. We want to stay in this realm but we slip, and as we slip we become jealous of those around us who still are flying high, then we get passionate and blindly start groping for what will get us back to that spot, but what we find is not enough and we think more is the answer and more and more, and in the end we fall. We cannot get back to that spot and so we rage and fume! We fall all the way back into hell. Thus the cycle of suffering begins again.

Getting Off the Hamster Wheel

Getting out of hell and making it all the way to the top realm is pointless because then you fall and you repeat it again and again, lifetime after lifetime. There is no lasting comfort in any of the realms. Sobriety breaks a portion of this cycle for us because we remove a portion of the cycle. We stop chasing that particular dragon. Sober living, in contrast to the darkest aspects of all those realms, puts us outside the cycle of our addiction. Pick up and we are right back on the wheel. This is why abstinence is the only true method when playing with our addiction, for we will always fall if we try to control or regulate our use. Of course the finer we live our life, the subtler the transitions from realm to realm. For some of us, just staying off the addiction wheel will be plenty, but we didn't get sober to be a glum lot. By working the steps and developing a spiritual life we refine our course through the realms. Sure, we will have moments, but they will not be as intense, last as long, or be as frequent.

Virtues and Riches

The enlightened warrior learns the virtues of the higher realms to help him (or her) along the way. These virtues are what the warrior cultivates as they continue along their path. Our discipline is not imposed from some outside force, but rather it occurs because we do not wish to repeat the way we were living. At first the discipline is difficult because it feels foreign but soon we discover that sober and clean we can take joy in this discipline. There are seven virtues of the higher realms that we continue to practice and strive to develop. These virtues are faith, discipline, generosity, learning, decency, modesty and wisdom. Those seven virtues lead to seven riches: nobility, good physical appearance, opulence, discriminating awareness (or prajna), splendidness, without sickness and longevity.

Without even exploring those seven virtues and seven riches, those words seem natural and beginning to manifest in our lives already. These riches are akin to the promises that the Big Book mentions as a result of the steps. Some of the Fifth Step promises are: that we can be alone at peace and ease, our fears fall from us, we feel close to the spirit of the universe, and that the drink problem may have disappeared. Surely these relate to where we are in our path of the dignities and we can see how the riches are beginning to manifest. Riches here do not necessarily mean financial riches and while our financial life may not be stellar, being free from our habit will improve our financial abilities quite nicely. We are beginning to change and that change will be apparent to many around us.

We have discussed faith in Step Three and discipline in Step Four, but we can still look at them here, for faith here is now manifesting in a sense of wholesomeness, togetherness and simplicity. Our faith is beginning to grow outward from a small seed into something that pervades our whole being. We have faith not only in our sobriety and the teachings but in our own existence as being good. When we look at discipline, now we see how our discipline of practice and the program have brought a sense of order in our lives. We are no longer resistant to the practice of meditation or attending meetings. We can enjoy the discipline because we see how the lack of discipline causes pain in those around us.

Generosity is not fundamentally tied to our wallets as typically inferred, but we are generous with the one thing we always have at hand, ourselves. We can be open, letting go of our need to hold ourselves back. We let go of much of that fear when we did the 5th step. Now we see that generosity is not so much about money but letting go. Learning is both the book smarts that we have been developing but also the experiential variety. Our experiences continue to grow so we continue to learn from our interactions with the world. We discover that we can do certain things in sobriety that we never thought possible.

We can conduct ourselves with a sense of decency. We are open and honest; we have a sense of integrity about ourselves and how we interact with the world. We are not looking to cheat the world anymore. Letting go of our need to control the outcomes and situations, we are dealing simply with the world. Decency grows as we lose our duplicitous nature. Since we are not trying to cheat the world or gain things that do not belong to us, we develop a sense of modesty. We know our sense of ego-driven pride nearly drove us to the grave, thus we know that whatever we are doing, we must hold that sense of modesty. Every action in the past was done from a calculated angle or a knee-jerk reaction. Now our actions start to come from our heart. When we do that we naturally begin to have a sense of modesty.

All of these things together begin to develop as wisdom. Sure, we are far from being the wise people we hope to be, but we are starting to have faith in our inner wisdom. This manifests as being able to see things differently; we have the bigger picture in mind. Those knee-jerk reactions start to leave us. As a result the mind of the warrior is perky, uplifted and accomplished. Our actions become simpler and more direct, with a sense of beauty and power.

The results are we experience the seven riches. Our faith turns into a sense of nobility, which comes from manifesting a good head and shoulders. This continues into a good physical appearance. Our appearance changes as we start living a healthier lifestyle. We are walking taller and feeling better. We start to feel a bit like the old days, like our youth has returned a bit. Generally not ingesting immense amounts of any substance will improve our physical wellbeing. When we are carrying ourselves better we develop a sense of opulence as a result of our general generosity. We still might not have much but what we have has a sense of richness about it; this is richness as compared to expensive. Prajna or wisdom develops from our learning. Combining that sense of richness and wisdom creates a splendidness which arises from our decency. Being modest, we take care of ourselves better, which manifests as being without sickness. Much of sickness is a result of negative energies in our bodies, so our practice eases those tensions as we let go and move through the world easier. As a result we experience longevity.

Finishing the Fifth Step we feel uplifted and perky like the Snow Lion. We are experiencing a new sense of freedom as we frolic in the cool, fresh highland air. The lion continually comes back to earth at the end of each jump. He is still bound to the earth. To free ourselves from habitual patterns and tendencies that were displayed in our Fourth Step, we need further work. Thus we continue on.

Step Six

Were entirely ready to have God remove all these defects of character.
(Big Book of AA)

Flying through the highland mountain air, leaping from mountaintop to mountaintop, the snow lion represents the joy and perkiness of the Shambhala warrior. The snow lion is perky because it is not caught in the traps of doubt and fear. We aren't always so lucky and the traps of doubt and fear will sometimes jump out and grab us, pulling us back down to Earth. That first moment when we were so high, working our program, having done the 5th step and feeling good--suddenly it's gone. We panic because we want that ease and comfort of the highland air and those virtues of the higher realms we discussed in Step Five. Yet what goes up must come down (for the most part) and thus we swing and get caught in the trap of doubt. Step Six looms before us like an impossible task. We get caught, stuck in doubt.

I mean come on, *entirely, ready,* and *all* are pretty strong words. Who would not have some doubts at this stage of the game? Even though we may feel wonderful and freer for having exposed our deep dark secrets, if we stopped right there the echoes of our dirty deeds would reverberate back to us time and time again. Yep, that's me; yep I threw up on my girlfriend that night, yep I stole money from kids piggy banks, yep I ran the car into the porch, on and on. We find ourselves getting caught in doubt that all this stuff is not really going to work. Where are those fifth step promises of being "alone in perfect peace and ease"? Some people in the rooms say that at this point the drink problem "was removed entirely" for them. While others like myself still had drinking on the brain quite often. Maybe it did go away for some people. Sure it worked for them, but we sometimes get the thought that this is not going to work for me.

Basic Sobriety

Addiction is as they say the only disease that tells you that you don't have the disease.

If at this point in your program, you still are fighting urges with your addiction, do not worry too much about it. The more I talked to people the more I understood that we all experience the "peace and ease" differently. I still felt a good deal crazy and sometimes very uncertain that this was all going to work for me. "A body badly burned by alcohol does not often recover overnight nor do twisted thinking and depression vanish in a twinkling." (Big Book of AA) There were definitely some doubts that lingered in my mind, very typical doubts.

When my wife and I would go to a concert I would see lots of people drinking and having what appeared to be a good time. My mind's first reaction is to remember those "good ole days" and want to be a part of it again. Taking a closer look at myself, I would realize those days were decades ago. Then when I looked a little closer at those people drinking and carrying on, I could see the desperation, fear and lack of joy in their eyes.

Each time we drift off from our breath on the cushion, we catch ourselves and remind ourselves of what we are doing and the instructions. "Alert before you daydream" is a slogan Trungpa coined. It is a natural tendency to drift off from our focus on sobriety. When that happens, we catch ourselves and we come back. At that point it is helpful to do a quick backwards scan through the steps. Is there something lurking I need to share, something bothering me, something I am trying to control, some old habit creeping up? Finally, touch on the bare reality of how bad it really was at the end, smashing the idea that you can safely drink, drug or do other substances like others.

So if you still feel a bit crazy after your fifth step? That is ok. While we feel better about having unloaded much of the weight we have been carrying, having to clean that mess up does not sound like a fun prospect. Yet having doubt can be a positive thing. The Buddha tells us that doubt is important. Unfortunately, since we have yet to fully develop the awareness of what we should accept and what we should reject, we can feel at a loss as to what to do. Knowing what to accept and what to reject is an intelligent and refined doubt, but we are not there yet. Here we are looking at the cool clear water; we are dying of thirst and we doubt that it will save us. This is a blind sense of doubt, an ignorant sense of doubt.

Doubt

Doubt is such a pervasive and detrimental thing, therefore the warrior needs to be free from doubt. That this doubt could be divided into six categories shows how it is not so simple and basic. The number one category of doubt is anxiety. This anxiety is based on the fact that we all suffer. We are not willing to let go of our ideas that do not work and listen to other ideas or concepts. The result is anxiety as we worry our fortress of ego may be penetrated or that our ideas are not sound. When we begin to feel that things aren't the way we like them to be, we doubt that they will ever be the way we want them to be. This manifests in jealousy as the second category. We doubt we are going to get what we need from the world. The third category is forgetfulness. We become so clouded by our doubt that we can't think, can't remember to have any sort of discipline. Life becomes haphazard and we become forgetful. To shore ourselves and our egos back up, to protect it, we become arrogant and project an extreme sense of self confidence. This arrogance and self-confidence is not based on anything but fear. It is a show. We doubt ourselves to the core. If someone does try to touch our doubt we slander everyone and everything. We doubt ourselves, believing our thoughts, ideas and actions are fabrications, but instead of allowing ourselves to admit that, we tear down anyone or any idea that tries to prove our lies. This all results in our inability to get our body and mind aligned.

In our addictions we have seen how doubt controlled our lives, ever the "egomaniac with an inferiority complex," and how it kept us mired in our habitual patterns. We doubted that anything could truly help us. We used that doubt and skepticism like a sword, cutting down ideas, concepts and people who threatened our fragile worlds. Thus doubt hid our fears from the world. This doubt became so subtle that we were fearful of anything beyond our immediate concept of the world, and that kept us trapped. We couldn't truly believe that it was possible to be in the world without our addictions. Doubt had such a hold on us that the only thing we could do was to keep on drinking or drugging. There was no way I was not going to get drunk two weeks from now at the Sunday barbeque, so it made no sense to get sober today.

Ultimately we doubted that we could exist in the world without our addiction. Without a drink in hand we could not exist in the world. The world would somehow collapse on us. We doubted that the world held everything we needed already. Therefore if we were not going to get from the world what we needed, then we were going to go out and take it. We doubted that the storms would pass and that the seasons followed one another. We believed only what we felt safe believing, and everything else was terrifying. We have seen how we wrapped ourselves in our cocoons, afraid to face the world because we doubted we could exist in the world clean and sober.

Doubting Basic Goodness

We have our laundry list of character defects and we falter, doubting that we can be anything but those items on that list. We were liars, cheats and thieves. At least at the moment we were sober liars, cheats and thieves but here were a lifetime of ingrained habits. In fact most of these habits were how we identified ourselves. Many of us have been told since a young age that we were worthless or unworthy, that we were selfish and self-centered, untrustworthy and bad. The more we believed that this was who we were the more we were apt to continue the negative karmic cycle of behaviors.

When we doubt our basic goodness we can excuse or justify all sorts of less than desirable behaviors. Believing ourselves to be bad, when faced with decisions or actions we easily went with the wrong type of behavior. We were no longer trying to live up to the good image people thought they were painting for us; we were living down to the image we had of ourselves.

A friend described how this played out in his life lay, as it lay hidden only to be discovered through sobriety and his spiritual path. *During an intense period of meditation the doubt began to bubble up. I doubted that I was worthy of the love I had in my life, whether it be from my children or from my wife. This doubt of being worthy of love has been a shadow that has followed my life. Doubting that I am worthy of the love given to me, I have acted in various ways which in turn drove love from my life. In some instances this resulted in jealous and controlling behavior, afraid to let love look in any other direction because if they did they would surely see how unworthy an object of affection I was. Terrified of losing the love in my life, I held on even tighter, in essence strangling love. I would try various means and methods to assure myself that this person truly loved me, or because I doubted myself I became overly affectionate or overly passionate, trying to prove that I was so much more worthy than anyone else. In still other instances it left me unappreciative and unable to see the love that was actually in my life. Doubting my own goodness caused me to doubt others' affections toward me. When the love I had in my life moved from the all–consuming, powerful new love, I did not understand that this was natural and so unnaturally tried to keep the love in that new love realm, always lamenting that things were not as they once were. I continually strived for something out there to make me feel good, feel loved, because I could not love myself, because I doubted my own inherent goodness.*

Kleshas

If we are not these character defects we have written down, who are we? What we see as lasting character defects, the Buddha described as obscurations of our mind, or kleshas. Kleshas are mental states which cloud the mind and manifest as unwholesome actions, our character defects. We have already been discussing some of the six kleshas in various forms. The six kleshas are Passion, Aggression, Ignorance, Greed, Envy and Pride, although sometimes listed as Desire, Anger, Pride, Ignorance, Doubt and View. According to the Buddha all our problems can be found in these six defilements. The good news is that as we develop our training we have the possibility to actually work with and through all the kleshas. Alcohol was but a symptom and it is within the kleshas we find many of the causes.

The first three are the root kleshas; the baseline emotions that drive us all are Passion, Aggression and Ignorance. We want to draw it in, push it away or be oblivious to it, whatever it may be. Usually, the passion and aggression were too much to handle and so we went right for the ignorance. We wanted to lose everything in that fog of ignorance. Passion is our desire, our wanting to feel good, to feel differently, to desire something or someone so greatly that we are completely consumed with them or it. Aggression is the reverse of the passion we can't possess, so we want to destroy those things that we cannot have or that threaten us. From these three simple base emotions all sorts of difficulties arise.

The next three are the more damaging ones as depicted in the 12x12, Pride, Jealousy and Avarice (i.e., greed). Pride is what the Big Book says is the root of our problem. Pride is "I." It is selfish and self centered. This is the root of our problems, always trying to come out ahead, to one up, to be better than the next person. From this grows our wonderful misused ego. Jealousy and envy is the thinking that the world isn't treating us fairly; the spouse, the boss, the coach are favoring someone else. In our minds we feel less than those around us, because we are trying to be better than them, except we are trying to be better than our false perception of them. This jealousy becomes claustrophobic, to the point where you can't breathe or think. Avarice is that even if we got what we wanted to be better than the other person, it wouldn't be enough; we want it all. We want more, and we don't want to let others have what we have. "All for me and none for you," older timer Ed, likes to say.

The good news is that these emotions are workable. They can be cut through, possibly even destroyed. This list, said in different words, would be akin to the seven deadly sins or the ten commandments. Almost everyone, in every time, has to deal with the power of their emotions. We are emotional beings. Many of us were probably overly emotional beings. Knowing our emotions are workable, that they are not solid and do not last forever, is a gift of wisdom to the alcoholic addict.

Working With Emotions

Emotions may seem to last forever. It sure has felt that we have hated that teacher for the last twenty years. As soon as we think of that person our blood starts to heat up and off we go. We went from happily walking along and some random thing reminds us of that teacher and boom, we are fuming again. Meditation, generally, will allow us to have some gaps in our emotional life. One method of dealing with a powerful emotion is by sitting through it. If you can separate the emotion from the story, then you can be fully present with the emotion. When we do that we will witness that each emotion has a beginning, middle and end. Without the story there is no air to fuel the flames. Without the story our emotions quickly die; of course letting go of the story is something we are not very good at. Letting go is something we have been working on since the moment we were told to just label our thoughts. Emotions are just thoughts on steroids, but we can let go of the story that fuels the emotion.

Another method of working with the kleshas is one that works with our awareness. We are aware we are angry at this person. We can again just be with the anger. However, instead of just working with the energy of the emotion, this time we work with the energy of the story and the energy of the emotion with a gentle inquisitiveness. With a sense of inquiry we can begin to explore the emotion. Where does it exist? Where does it reside in our body? Where is the center of the emotion? Is the cause something we are experiencing right now, or is it something in the past or future? Does the klesha abide in me or the other person? Does it reside in one of my senses? Where does it come from and where does it go?

The answers to these questions allow us to take some of the juice out of the emotion. We can't quite put a finger on it. We can't quite locate it. The more we look, the less we find. The room that we thought was filled with anger is empty. This is a core realization, one we will forget easily and often--that these emotions that once ruled our lives are empty.

Unfortunately, sometimes the energy of emotions is so strong and overwhelming that they feel solid, as if all you are is anger or jealousy or pride. Some are so subtle, like arrogance; even when it's not completely obvious it is still there. With awareness we work with whatever is going on. It is awareness that catches us in the midst of the klesha. We work on fine-tuning our awareness. Remember, we have been using these habits, these so-called defects of character, for many years, if not lifetimes. The beginning is simply becoming willing to be aware of them.

Character Defects and Mindfulness

Before we can become completely willing to let go of any defect of character we really need to take the time to become aware of our behaviors. Steps Six and Seven seem to echo the same concept in how we begin to work with ourselves. We have taken care of our physical sobriety, once we have put down our addiction of choice. The kleshas are the emotional states that fluctuate between the highs and lows. Addiction attacks us through our body, mind, and spirit. If we do not change all three aspects of ourselves, we are likely to return to our addictive behaviors, or as a friend likes to say, "If we only put down the drink, then we still have 2/3rds of the problem."

Step Six is an indicator light of our sobriety. When I start acting in my character defects, I know that something just ain't right. Sometimes the indicator light is obvious: ice cream at 7am, I probably need to call my sponsor or another person in recovery. Other indicators may be more difficult to spot, like a repetitive mental phrase use. Before we entered a program of recovery we hardly noticed the tendency to behave or act in these defects. We ignored any indicators or warnings. Maybe we have heard people tell us that we drank too much, that we were selfish or self-centered and that was about as deep as we got with our character defects in the past. Now, if we are to have a lasting sobriety we need to be aware of our behaviors. Once we become aware of our behaviors we have a chance but first we have to notice that we are doing them.

This is why a regular sitting practice is so important, even at this phase of our sobriety. Having developed a solid foundation of meditation using shamatha, mindfulness of our breathing, we now begin to pair it with vipashyana or insight. When we do this we begin to develop awareness. At first we use others to help us have some sense of awareness. We listen in meetings, we share, we get advice. When we first make phone calls to people we barely know we are asking for them to help save our lives. They are, usually, more than glad to listen and help us see what we cannot see. We have not had much practice acting sanely and so we turn to others to help us see our behavior when we are not aware.

What we get when we turn to these other members of our fellowship is usually not what we want to hear. It is usually the right course of action. Inwardly we often know the answers already; they were just not the answers that we wanted to hear. In the moments that we do not have awareness of ourselves, our motives or the situation, we turn to others who have more practice at being aware of the bigger picture. Before sobriety our general course of action was "me, me and more me." The Big Book talks about the director syndrome. The director is only aware of his vision, what he thinks will make the play right. When the play is the way he wants it, it will produce happiness for all. However, it usually does not go that way. We reach out to others to help us learn to have awareness of the bigger picture. That picture is generally our sobriety. Therefore we are looking for their awareness to help us navigate our sobriety; we are not looking at how to wrest happiness out of every situation.

Basic Sobriety

These sober elders provide us with another way of looking at the situation or another course of action. It may be difficult to hear, it is often not what we want to hear, and chances are if we are listening to the right people, we too will navigate sobriety long enough to generate our own awareness of the bigger picture.

Through meditation we have been plowing the field so that insight may be planted. We have returned to our breath over and over again. We have practiced letting go of our thoughts. No thought was a gold star thought, and whether it was a good thought or bad thought, it did not matter; we let them go. But if we just kept sitting there, only fixating on letting go of all thoughts, where would we be? Would we be dumb meditators or zombie-like beings or blissed-out idiots? If we held too tightly to the process of shamatha, not progressing, we would be creating in meditating what we found in our addictions--a way to avoid the world. We drank and drugged, ate or slept around, so that we would not have to feel what we are feeling. We sought to avoid everything and we could use meditation to accomplish that as well. Thus as we develop the ability to stay with our breath, to not get carried off with our thoughts, we need to begin to open to insights.

Contemplating the teachings opens us up to insight and this provides awareness as to the true nature of the world. We are plowing the field and planting some seeds. We begin to contemplate the dharma and our experiences with the dharma. Settling our mind through meditation has allowed us to see clearer. We have let go (of some of) our passion, aggression and ignorance. We are more logical and direct. Now we begin to feel a sense of our body, and that sense of our body is more dreamlike, more romantic and more empty. We are aware of our "self" and thus we can begin to contemplate that self. We can contemplate our experiences. We can taste our experiences and thoughts while still maintaining a sense of nonattachment about them.

It is this awareness that holds the key to working our defects of character. Awareness helps us to learn how to handle ourselves and our lives. The first thing we become aware of is how awkward and uncomfortable we are, physically and mentally. Previously we felt something and mindlessly sought a way to alleviate that feeling of unease. Our goal is to develop an awareness of ourselves such that we can begin to loosen the grip of our defects of character on our lives.

Completing our 5th step may have been the first time that we became aware of the patterns of behaviors in our lives. We only took each moment or event as a single moment, not connected to the bigger picture of our lives or the world around us. When we look at all our resentments, our relationships, deeds and fears, we can see before us patterns of our behaviors. We find our ways of dealing with the world. Every time A happened I did B and then C occurred. When we only looked at one instance of our life, it may not have registered that it was part of a larger pattern. Laying it all out, the patterns are easily seen. Unfortunately, "self-knowledge avails us nothing." Being armed with these facts about ourselves means little unless we become aware of these actions. Vipashyana helps us process this information.

Character Defect Awareness

We begin by paying attention to our character defects. Each morning, we can start with an aspiration to be aware of a certain character defect. Then we watch for that character defect through the day. In the beginning we find ourselves realizing our actions after we have gone through them in their entirety. As we acquire more awareness we start to catch ourselves earlier and earlier. Next we catch ourselves caught in the moment of following the flow of the defect. Maybe at that moment we can cut the flow and stop acting in the defect of character. Catching ourselves earlier and earlier, soon we start to catch the first thoughts of the defect. We start to see the thought arise. Our awareness allows us to see the bigger picture of the moment, knowing that the small thought will manifest in our acting in our character defects.

Basic Sobriety

Each morning we can vow to not act in our character defects, and this is no easy task. As we begin to look deeper and deeper into these "defects" we discover we are really looking at the "of character" aspect. These defects are a part of me. Sure, I'm willing to give up some of the bigger, grosser defects but most of them I really like. Until they start to cause enough pain in our life, we are willing to keep them hanging around. Once we reach a certain pain threshold, only then do we say, "I better stop this behavior." To do this is downright uncomfortable. We are asking ourselves to live in that uncomfortable state. We may take a defect like lying and say, "Ok, I stopped lying so I'm good" but then we realize that we are not always completely honest; we find ourselves living in many gray areas. The finer and finer we push the point, the more we may see how we are lying to ourselves about the world and our experiences. We need to keep pushing forward. As we may have a handle on one defect another pops up, or as a friend used to say, "Your defects of character never go away; they just go off stage and change costumes."

It is hard to know which character defects are bad or good. What I believe we are going for is a middle ground here. It is not that we need to get rid of all the pieces of our character all at once; we just need to hold the middle, to not get completely wrapped up in the emotion or defect. Our goal is to become complete human beings. We as addicts just seem to take everything to the extreme. We generally seem to focus all our energy in a particular direction; we are all-in kind of people. We need that one thing which we never seemed to have, balance. When His Holiness the Karmapa was once asked, "Which is more important to focus on, helping others or working on ourselves through meditation?" His Holiness responded, "Whichever one you feel you are lacking." We need to find balance.

For most of us our erratic emotions are what keep us from finding a sense of balance in our lives. Learning to work with the energy of our emotions is one of the keys to freedom from our habitual behaviors, learning to accept ourselves where we are in each moment. No feeling is ultimately bad and no feeling is ultimately good, but becoming aware of our feelings connects us with our true nature and all of humanity. Acknowledging our emotions, that we are emotional beings, with defects and assets, is important in the development of the Shambhala warrior. Casting off all our emotions or feelings, we would achieve zombie-like results. This is not the goal of recovery or meditation, nor are we looking for a blissed-out trip. The more we can connect with our feelings and emotions the more we can connect with the world around us. The world around us had a hand in creating each emotion, such that if we can learn to relate properly with the emotion, we can learn to relate properly and directly with the situation or moment.

When we are relating properly to our emotions, we are properly and directly dealing with the world around us. Many of our irrational fears are based on this improper relationship to the world around us. The beginning of that distorted relationship, for many, is our disconnected sense of self. I am basing my emotions and feelings on the world around me, but when I spend my time in the realm of the intellect and ego, i.e., my head, I am not in direct relationship to the world. I am relating to the world based on my filters and concepts. When we are in emotional distress it is important to ground our bodies, to connect with the earth, while allowing ourselves the space of the heavens above. We must come back to our body in times of emotional distress, to connect with what is really going on.

It was our unrealistic relationship with our emotions that created many of our habitual patterns and causes of our addictions. We need to now work toward creating a proper relationship with the world around us. The moment a lasagna hits the table I am immediately filled with fear and panic. This is not relating properly with reality. Lasagna is not going to conk me on the head or eat me like a tiger. What I am panicked about, or terrified about, is a series of past experiences and future projections. I am aggressively trying to push this moment away instead of relating with the reality at hand. There is no need to break into a cold sweat when faced with a lasagna. Yet there I am, caught and pulled, hooked by my kleshas. If I could be gentle with myself, not berate myself for this silly fear of lasagna, and begin to question this lasagna, this moment, What am I feeling now? My skin? My eyes? I can begin to see that nothing in that moment is creating those feelings. If I pay attention to what is actually going on, there will be a different set of feelings and emotions developing. I can begin to relate with this lasagna and how it tastes, not what I think it will taste like, or how it tasted 30 years ago, but what it actually tastes like now. Then I may actually enjoy the moment, the taste, smells, etc.

When we properly feel our body and our experiences, we deal directly with reality. We can touch our goodness when we are connected to all our experiences and senses.

Dignity

In the third step, we in essence said we are going to get out of our own way. When we remove our defects of character, what will we discover? When we looked at emotions, little by little we discover they are empty of content. If we follow the logic then I am empty of content, as well as my whole life, which was made up of the story that revolves around those emotions. The Heart Sutra, a popular piece of Buddhist scripture, reminds us that form is emptiness and emptiness is form, that we are empty and full at the same time. If we can get rid of the pieces that obscure our true nature, what will we find? Sure, ultimately it may be enlightenment, but what we begin to find under all those defects of character is a sense of purity. We touch the basic goodness within us that has always remained unstained and that manifests as a sense of dignity. Let me repeat that: our basic goodness within us has always remained unstained.

As humans we have a natural sense of dignity which we can connect to through our practice and our sobriety. Give an alcoholic a bottle of vodka and he will show you what undignified looks like. Yet the truth is that almost all people, those with the "ism" and those without, are all running around without a sense of their own dignity. They are blown about by the kleshas and confused about their true natures. Working, eating, driving, having sex, walking in the woods, writing poetry, watching reality TV, having babies and killing each other--so many activities on both sides of the spectrum carried out by well-meaning people, disconnected from their own sense of dignity and self-worth. We can naturally begin to discover that we have an inherent dignity and confidence. We can carry ourselves with dignity, regardless of our place in the world. We respect ourselves and that becomes respecting others. Suddenly our whole world becomes filled with a sense of dignity. There is never a moment off, so we can't separate the preparing a fine meal from eating it or from cleaning up the dishes afterwards. It can all have a sense of dignity about it.

We connect to our dignity by working with our emotions. We are no longer afraid to face the world. We are free from doubt and fear because we can overcome our emotions without aggression. The warrior of Snow Lion is able to work with both faults and virtues and knows that our inherent virtues far exceed our temporal and temporary faults. The warrior of Snow Lion has awareness, so that he is working with whatever arises within him. As a result he can begin to extend that kindness and gentleness to others. When we first began sitting we received a subtle transmission of posture, of sitting with our backs straight and our head uplifted. We aligned our head and shoulders. In that moment we touched our goodness and felt that sense of dignity. That sense of dignity is always there for us to connect with.

When we connect with that sense of dignity, we start to perceive the simple logic of the world. We no longer wear lampshades on our heads, not just because we are sober, but because we start to see the simple logic of our world. The seasons follow each other; summer does not come after fall and winter does not come before summer, but they flow as is needed. The world today tries to break that logic with the 24 hour a day, 7 days a week mentality; we can now eat breakfast for dinner and have fresh strawberries regardless of the season. Fifty-two weeks a year I can eat strawberries with my breakfast; there is never a time that I cannot walk into a market and get "fresh" strawberries. We see people wearing socks on their hands and pants hanging below their knees. Billboards tell us about plastic surgeons and freezing away fat. If you don't like the weather in the North, come to the South and when you do not like the weather in the South you go back North again. We have ignored the simple logic of the world. We have lived without connection to our own dignity for much too long. It is proper to clean up our kitchen after we eat, to pick up our clothes from the floor, to make our beds. We do these things at first to start working with the mess we have made in our lives, then we do them because it is the proper thing to do. We can now invite friends over and not be ashamed. We start to uplift the world around us and the world starts to uplift us in return.

To dress properly, to carry ourselves in a dignified manner, to enjoy the world around us are fundamental to the idea that there is no separation between the outer world and the inner world. How we treat one is a manifestation of the other.

Can we have celebrations in sobriety? Of course we can, but most of us when we first get sober worry that we will not be able to celebrate again, or in other words we cannot imagine a celebration without alcohol. I frequently hear newcomers lament that they will not be able to toast at their children's weddings or enjoy a sporting event. Holidays were not viewed as celebrations, but free passes to drink all we wanted. Weddings were not about the bride and groom but about the open bar. The list goes on and on. Yet when we bring this sense of dignity and celebration to our life, our lives become filled with celebrations great and small.

I enjoyed painting, but I also enjoyed the beer and cigarettes I allowed myself to "indulge" in while painting, to where the painting would get lost to the drinking. I feared that I would not be able to paint without a drink and a smoke. When I finally got the courage to paint again, sober, I cried. I was so overcome with the joy of painting, sober and fresh. This was a celebration. Each time I paint I feel that sense of joy and happiness. Creating, enjoying our world, relating properly to one another--this is what celebration is about, not the kegger we thought was a celebration before. When we celebrate life, we do so with a sense of dignity and humility. We can bring that sense of celebration to every aspect of our life. Every aspect of our life can have a sense of dignity.

When we have dignity we can begin to accept who we are without our habitual patterns. Awareness helps us see which habitual patterns we should accept and which ones to reject, which ones we are doing just to be seen as good little boys and girls and which ones are fundamentally positive. We can learn to accept our feelings in each moment. It's ok to be angry. It's ok to be sad. We no longer degrade ourselves by acting in these energies. Everything is workable. It is ok to be Frank or Sally or whoever we are and it is ok to be ourselves, warts and all. When we approach this world from a fundamental base of goodness, not from an affirmational way of trying to trick ourselves to believe that we are good, our lives start to have a sense of discipline and balance. We don't need to have fancy clothes or furnishings; we can wear what we have and live with dignity. A sense of joy and humor comes from not being continually thrown around by our own emotions; instead, we are able to dance with them. We can ride our emotions like a dignified king on his beautiful horse. We are starting to sense an energy within.

With dignity we have awareness of our character defects and we have the discipline and confidence to work with whatever arises. We have glimpsed the emptiness of our emotions, which allows us to find some peace within us. When we connect with our emotions, with who we are in each moment, we can connect with all other beings. Each of us is constantly working with a never-ending barrage of kleshas, but being aware of them within ourselves, we can see them in others. As they are workable within ourselves, they also are workable with others.

Basic Sobriety

This natural dignity is very simple and very direct. Take a deep breath: in that moment you straighten up your shoulders and your head naturally rests there uplifted and aligned. You cannot take a deep breath all slouched over and crooked. Just that simple action is a lightning bolt of wakefulness.

Step Seven

Humbly asked him to remove our shortcomings. (Big Book of AA)

True victory is to win without having to go to battle at all. The question becomes, do we have to do battle with ourselves to be something we are not? To which the answer is no, because we are trying to become what we truly already are. In the Sixth Step we looked and became ready to let go of our character defects and in the Seventh Step we are asking to remove our shortcomings. Many people look at their nature as solid and unchanging, that they cannot change. Is this not ego at its very best? So let's start there. "I cannot change" is a story that we oh-so-dearly wanted to hold onto while we were active in our addiction. It is not so much the change that we fear; it's the fact that we are afraid of losing the "I". What if I dropped the story I told myself?

The Stories We Tell Ourselves

One summer at Shambhala Mountain Center, I found myself standing at the edge of circle awaiting the opening ceremony. I usually prefer the back or edge of any crowd. *I don't feel comfortable among people,* I tell myself. When I first signed up for the program I requested a single tent. I wanted to be by myself, as far away from others as I could be. The reason I told myself, and others, was that I snore and I did not want to disturb other people. I believe in the idea of enlightened society, just let me work on it from the fridge or behind the scenes. I am not good with people, I am shy, I don't like making small talk are all the reasons I tell myself. I, I, I. When I found myself talking to two other "introverts," joking and laughing about how we could not be social with a group of people... well, at least those non-introverted social people over there, I have to ask myself is that story really true? While I may not have wanted to be a part of those people over there that I saw as different from me, I very much wanted to find those like me, at that moment other "introverts" and later other drunks and addicts. The schedule had a recovery group meeting the second night of the program and once more the following week. After that first meeting the group asked the coordinator of the Heart of Recovery at the program if we could meet every night that there was not something official on the schedule for dinner. While I tell myself I want to be alone, that I do not like talking to and being around people, I also know I need and want to be with people.

In the beginning of our addiction there was a story about ourselves and the story of what drugs and alcohol did for us. We probably were not even aware of it then but there was a story, and for me alcohol helped me blur the edges of those stories. I am shy around women. I don't fit in with other guys because I am too smart and sensitive--two stories that I believed only held true for me. Thus to be around other people, to ask women out, I needed what alcohol gave me the confidence to do. I went to an all-boys Catholic high school, so that made my insecurities about women and my Jewish self even more dramatic. When there were ski trips or school dances, I definitely needed alcohol to make me be other than who I really was. College, same scenario. Other stories arose but regardless the cure, remedy and solution was, for me, always alcohol.

What followed from the initial story--that alcohol makes me better than I am--transformed over time into the addiction belief that without alcohol I cannot function. Yet here we are now at Step Seven and maybe a few twenty-four hours under our belts. We have firsthand experience that the story about not being able to function without our addiction does not hold true. The first trip to the grocery store sober was pretty terrifying. In the beginning entering that maze of multicolored products and people without a solid defensive buzz was terrifying, but now I can go to the grocery store without the fear that a case of beer will jump into my cart and then force itself down my throat. The seventh step is asking us to take the logic further. The seventh step is asking, "What happens if you drop all the stories?"

What happens if we drop the stories? If I stop telling myself all those irrational fears that I wrote down and then told my sponsor about in Steps Four and Five, then what? What if I dropped the story that I am not good with people? What if I dropped the story that I am shy? We each have a thousand stories. Some of the stories are at the surface and some are hidden deep down inside. Not only do those stories misrepresent the world out there but worse, we believe that these stories are truly who we are. The question is, can I change?

I won't lie, I still hate being around people much of the time. I still hang to the edge and I make up all the reasons why I don't like you and why you won't like me. Most days I still have an icy demeanor, but I believe that can change. Now there are moments of warmth and lightness, where there was only ice and dark. The 12x12 asks us if we can change our addiction, why can we not change other aspects of ourselves? I am not going to stand here and tell you that you can do this in 5 minutes a day and rah-rah-rah, hocus pocus. It is not easy, but you can do it. When I tell you that you can change, it's not because I have drunk the Kool-Aid, but because I have been down the road. My sponsor describes it as doing a 180 with our lives. It is not magical and mystical, but you can teach an old dog new tricks. When I say you can, I do want you to believe me; I want you know that it is possible, but you need to see for yourself if these tools will work for you as well.

No Magic Pills

When I first began meditating, I wanted a magic elixir of practices and spiritual voodoo that would help me handle life, the sins of my past and the fears of the future. I thought if I just did A, B, and C that the result would be bliss. Unfortunately that was the same mentality that kept me drinking for many, many years. If I could just find the correct proportions of beer, whiskey, cigarettes, pills, sex and work, then I could manage and enjoy life. The problem was that it was a moving target of what proportions were needed on any given day and I always shot way past what was needed. Trying to do the exact same thing with my spiritual practices was only going to lead to failure. I was looking for a magic wand or a silver bullet.

The Big Book tells me that one day my spiritual condition will fail, and that only working with another alcoholic will save the day. In my mind I needed to be prepared for my spiritual condition failing. What will happen on that day that the boss yells at me, the ex-wife is mad at me, the kids are driving me crazy, the car gets a flat and I didn't get a good night's sleep? Whatever the ingredients were going to be, I knew that a day would come where my spirituality failed me because at that time I could barely handle just one of those things at a time. This is not to say that spirituality would actually fail me, but I would fail to use it. In the beginning, I tried a number of different techniques. Talking to another alcoholic and going to meetings surely saved the day when prayer, running, painting, yelling, breaking things, and anger didn't quite cut it. Those were the tools I had for use to deal with my emotions and I was not getting "better" as quickly as I would have liked. I was far from happy, joyous and free. My emotions were still wildly erratic. Part of the problem was I was trying to "control" my emotions, which is a losing proposition. I needed a better antidote for my emotions because there would come a moment when I could not get to a gym, my studio, the track, a meeting, a phone, etc.

Wisdom Energies

All emotional energy is workable. Whether that energy is within us or coming from out there, it is workable. Emotional energy did not feel workable in the beginning. It was huge and powerful and needed to be actualized and released. Without drugs and alcohol that energy felt hugely overwhelming at times. Each of us has a habitual way of dealing with the energies within us and the world around us. Anger is definitely by far my most common method for dealing with the world, but not my only one.

Since good or bad is merely a story we overlay on any situation or emotion, these energies are typically named the Five Wisdom Energies or the Five Buddha Families. With wisdom, the energy of one form may be transmuted into another form. These wisdom energies relate to all manner of things like colors, seasons, directions, and elements. Basically, any aspect of the phenomenal world can be described by one or more of these energies. We will focus on the energy of emotions and neurotic patterns. Vajra is the word associated with the energy of anger. The other four are Ratna, which is associated with the energy of pride; Padma, which is associated with the energy of passion; Karma, which is associated with the energy of jealousy and envy; and Buddha, which is associated with the energy of dullness.

Typically, we have one primary type of neurotic pattern that we use to deal with the world, but there may be hints of the others as well in every moment. We may experience anger and jealousy, passion and pride, anger with passion and on down the list, with some or all of the different energies playing out within us. Since every moment has the ability to wake ourselves up, even these "negative" energies have wisdom in them. What we learn first is that there is a possibility of changing the energies, like an alchemist turning lead to gold, only here we are turning anger into wisdom, or envy into accomplishment. This is the beginning of learning to deal with energies, neurotic habits or shortcomings, learning that they too are workable. In AA parlance if "God is all or nothing" then it is not that anger is not God and wisdom is God; Anger and wisdom are two faces of the same coin.

In Step Six we looked at our character defects as the actions that we took to deal with the thoughts and emotions we were feeling. As a result we lied, cheated, stole, etc. By first becoming aware of and then realizing we were performing all these actions we could now look at where they come from and how to work with the underlying energies in Step Seven. Since anger is my habitual pattern of dealing with the world, the resulting actions were rage, destruction, hurt feelings, hurtful words and actions. Vajra energy is associated with anger, it is very blunt and direct, and it can also be defensive or aggressive or sharp and clear. This energy can be transmuted into a "Mirror-like Wisdom". Vajra means indestructible. There is a great deal of wisdom to found in our anger; we just need to learn to process and deal with that energy in more skillful ways. Anger can have intelligence, letting us know that something is wrong, that something needs to change. Unfortunately, righteous anger and self-righteous anger have only a fine line between them and we made ill use of both in our addictions. When anger is transmuted into wisdom it does so when we can look at all the corners of the situation, seeing the relationship of one element to another, or as the Big Book reminds us we need to "pause when agitated."

Pride should be characterized with stealing, it causes so much harm, says AA literature. Pride is associated with Ratna, the creation of a completely secure and solid "I". This solid and secure "I" is always in danger of falling apart so there is always a sense of anxiety and worry. However, the wisdom when we transmute pride is equanimity, a sense of calm and evenness of temper. When we are off the "me plan" we are able to connect with the world around us. This sense of calm comes from the fact that we understand that "I" can never be solid and secure. We learn to accept the emptiness and general insecurity of a world that is not exactly what it appears to be.

Another affliction of so many of us addicts and alcoholics is a sense of passion, which is not so much lust but the grasping quality of passion. We wanted to draw it all into us. There is always a sense of wanting more. Here in Padma it is a sense of wanting to possess completely rather than to just be united with someone or something. Our passions for fame, possessions and people took on hysterical and neurotic proportions. It has a rich and sultry feel. Our passion is a path of self-destruction, ultimately leading to the realization of the destruction of our passion, since we know that nothing outside of ourselves can ever fulfill our desire completely and utterly. As you hear in the rooms, one day I would do anything for another drink and the next day I would do anything not to drink. Within passion is the wisdom of "Discriminating Awareness", the wisdom to see distinctly the difference between this and that, and to be aware of what to accept and what to reject. Our passions are not evil if we are connected to the wisdom within them. They can lead us to love, to freedom, and joy when we don't become all consumed by them. Padma excites the senses and can be the birth of art and inspiration.

Karma is associated with jealousy and envy, but jealousy and envy taken up a few notches. Trungpa calls it "Absolute Paranoia". Even when we are not experiencing the all-too-much fun, drug-induced paranoia or the paranoia of guilt, we can be caught up in a constant state of comparison and envy. We feel that others will get what we want first and that there will be none left for us. As a result we will be irritated by others' successes and accomplishments. In AA jargon, we are comparing our insides with others' outsides, which results in everyone's life, spouse, job, kids, family, vacations, looking greater and more wonderful than ours (thank you, social media). Thus life becomes a constant state of looking over our shoulders to see if what others have is greater than what we have. Transmuting that sense of paranoia, we find the wisdom of "All-Accomplishing Action". Developing a proper relationship to the world, we can go out and accomplish what needs to be accomplished. What we truly need, we can achieve because we can direct our actions and energy appropriately. If we can drop the paranoia and purely place 100% of our mental faculties on the tasks at hand, how much more productive would we be?

While in our addictions, many of us became very familiar with the quality of dullness in the Buddha wisdom family. We were weighed down by doubt, procrastination and laziness. I did what I needed to do and that was about it, enough to get by. We did not want to see the truth of the world and so we ignored it, lost and crushed by the weight of our own search for oblivion and relief. This heaviness and dullness, in which there seems to be no possible action, is related to the Buddha wisdom energy, of All-Encompassing

Basic Sobriety

Space. Where the world only seems filled with darkness and misery, the world can be filled with possibility and space. Anything can truly happen. The Buddha wisdom is the ground for all the other wisdoms. It is at the center of the other four, allowing the space for all the others to arise. When we experience the wisdom of this energy we are easygoing and accepting, everything has the space to occur and it's ok.

The importance in all of this is that we can accept our emotions. Emotions are not evil and bad. Learning to work with our emotions instead of running from them is the key to being human. We are human and we feel. There is no getting around that. The fact that we feel leads many of us to try to feel only a particular way or ward off certain emotions. We can learn to feel properly and fully. Yes, early in sobriety when we get that initial rush of emotions, they feel like a tidal wave because we have opened the dam and released the floodgates. Now we can have a more relaxed spaciousness about our emotions. Learning to flow with our emotions, to not be carried off by them, is key to our maintaining our sobriety.

The Garuda

We are learning to relate to ourselves as we are and as we truly are. As we truly are is a wellspring of basic goodness, filled with energy and ability. The warrior of Shambhala is outrageous in his behaviors and actions. Here we are not saying that we are wild and crazy. No, we are outrageous because we have developed enough discipline and humility to step beyond our comfort zone. The symbol for this is the Garuda. The Garuda is said to be born fully grown, hatched in space with no need to touch the earth; it soars in the vastness of the sky. The Garuda is outrageous because it does not need any reference points. It does not even have the reference point of earth. Therefore the warrior of Shambhala renounces anything that comes between himself and the world. To do this we must avoid the trap of hope. We have avoided all the categories of doubt; now we must avoid hope. We avoid hope because it is based on ego and securing ego's domain, that in the future everything will be ok. The five traditional categories of hope to be avoided are poverty mentality, biasedness, aggression, passion and trying to measure the space of our mind.

While hope in general seems like a positive word, there is a flip side of hope which expresses a lack of what we are. It is something we do not have and we hope we get it; as a result we are poor in our own minds. We are not getting the love we want or the right kind of love. With Step Seven we are learning humility, which is the opposite of poverty mentality. Poverty mentality is thinking that what we have is not good enough. Humility is having a proper relationship to what we have in our life. With humility we are learning to work with the world through a sense of openness.

Biasedness is a big one in the rooms of recovery. Usually we take sides with ourselves, or whatever outcome we hope for. We want to have a way. We hope that by doing all these things, all our meditation and meetings, working with others and being good, that the universe will look at us favorably. Our bias runs in rivers great and small and our emotional state is hinged to the outcomes of these biases. We need to learn to do the work, regardless of the outcome, or to be able to enjoy the game for the game, not for who wins or loses. Tied to that sense of biasedness is a sense of aggression; we begin to attach resentments to whether our side wins or loses. We know there will be an outcome but the chance of it going against our desires or hopes causes us to react with aggression.

If we achieve what we hoped for, the outcome came the way we hoped, we develop passion for the achievement. We get all gooey in it. Trying to take in as much of the victory as we can, but knowing that it will never be enough, we start to falter and realize that our victory was short-lived and now we begin to feel defeated.

These levels of hope progress as a result of our meditation and sobriety, of our own awareness, so that we go from being conscious of our poverty mentality all the way to the spaciousness before ego found something to hope for. Once we discover spaciousness in our minds, we want to quantify it, to show it off, to judge and compare it. We try to measure our minds, our achievements. We have found the vastness and begin to have hope that we can reach the edges so that we can get some reference points. We have reached a level of hope where the mighty Garuda soars, in the spaciousness of our mind without limits. The Garuda soars with no goal, whereas we find ourselves looking for a destination. We find the space of our mind so self-congratulatory we feel we must be really getting somewhere to have found this space.

Renunciation

Giving up hope is not the same as hopelessness. We gave up our hope of overcoming our addictions by direct assault when we reached a state of hopelessness. The result of that hopelessness was victory and freedom from addiction. Traps of hope are chains we need to break along the route of our sobriety. It is perhaps too much at times to be completely out there in that open space. Little by little we learn to start to move forward without the need for the hurrahs and back slaps. We are learning to be clean and sober, for the sake of being clean and sober. If we can work with what is arising, the world will respond with the results. It is the self-serving hopes that we must be on the lookout for, the ones that shore up ego's territory.

Learning to let go of the results of our actions is very difficult. Our entire society seems geared toward results. Society tells us that results are the only thing that matter. Win at all costs. When we first came to recovery, most of us hoped for very specific results (usually very foolish ones like how to drink and/or drug responsibly). We want the promises to come true. If we did certain actions, we should get certain results. We are hoping for a peaceful, serene and happy sobriety. Yet these hopes are a trap. It is going to take some time before we are able to let go of the results. Most of us are not good at putting anything down, or as we typically think of it, quitting.

Renunciation is the rejection of something, typically a belief or course of action. In recovery we are renouncing something that is causing us pain and trouble. The warrior renounces anything that keeps us from experiencing the world, which is good, because I cannot quit anything. I could never quit drinking or smoking or doughnuts, no matter how much I hoped, prayed and begged for it, nor however hard I tried. The Big Book says, "When this sort of thinking is fully established in an individual with alcoholic tendencies, he has probably been placed beyond human aid, and unless locked up, may die or go permanently insane." The Big Book also talks about how the desire to drink just up and leaves, that it is no longer an issue that "it has disappeared completely." Remember, we never quite quit drinking, we only have a daily reprieve.

When I quit drinking, I did not say "tomorrow I will quit" or set a "quit date" like those stop smoking ads used to say. Any time I set a quit date for smoking, I needed to chain smoke a pack the night before, completely upping my addiction and therefore needing it all the more the next day. When I quit smoking, I just put it off for that day. I still had a carton and half in my night stand. Drinking was much the same--just get through this day and we can revisit the thought of drinking tomorrow. Strangely enough, I had my last drink on the Friday before Super Bowl Sunday. What fool does that? At that moment all I could think was *I just can't do it another day.* I did not think or say, "That's it; I quit!" Early in sobriety when I would think of not drinking for any length of time into the future, I would get sick to my stomach, as waves of nausea accompanied the dread of "never drinking again." A phrase I hear a lot in the rooms is, "You can always drink tomorrow." We put off taking a drink, just for today, then repeat ad infinitum. This is why we do it only for one day at a time. A lifetime is too much for us. Sometimes fifteen minutes is too much for us. As it's said in the rooms, "Try it. Go to 90 (meetings) in 90 (days), get a sponsor, work the steps, see how it feels. If you want to go back to drinking after that, we'll gladly refund your misery."

Basic Sobriety

Renunciation is a gentle letting go. Quitting is hard and fast, while renunciation is the middle way of letting go. With renunciation we try to maintain a sense of balance. We don't struggle too hard, nor do we just give in. If we slip and return to a bad habit we don't just dive in deeper and deeper, swimming to the bottom. If we slip, just like in meditation we return to our aspiration to be free of the behavior, thought or habit that we wish to let go of. We do this with a sense of gentleness. If we shame ourselves for slipping we just compound one problem with another. Right from the start we need to renounce shaming ourselves. Some of these habits have been building for decades, or lifetimes, so we need to be gentle with ourselves when we do slip back into old behaviors. "It is ok to feel angry. It is just not ok to act in that anger" is a mantra of mine during trying times. I have been fortunate to have accepted my life as an alcoholic with one white chip (and I pray my only) but when the thought to drink does come back up my sponsor in his gentle way reminds me, "Alcoholics think about alcohol, but alcohol kills alcoholics."

When many of us generally think of quitting we think it is all black or all white; if we get into gray areas or "fail", we add to our misery by thinking ourselves losers, failures, etc. Our Western society has been shoving that idea down our throats constantly. A politician, actor or leader who hides skeletons is shamed and thrown to the wolves for their shortcomings. That is why in many ways while the aspiration is similar; renouncing something is gentler than quitting. Thich Nhat Hanh reminds us, if we cut the power to a fan it is still going to take a while for it to come to a complete stop. If we stumble, we come back to our intent as quickly as we can and begin again from there. There are "no mistakes." We start from right where we are at each and every moment, and in the best of those moments we can keep our aspirations headed in the right direction.

The farther we move along the more we discover about ourselves. The more we discover about ourselves the more we discover layers of habitual neuroses and shortcomings. Step Seven asks to have these shortcomings removed. To be ready to remove these shortcomings, to let them go, to renounce them, we must continue to develop egolessness. We must continue to sit and learn, to continue our practice of letting go of our thoughts. The farther we go along, the more strings of the cocoon we discover that need to be cut. Sometimes we do so with solemn vows, but the Warrior of Shambhala doesn't need to be so rigid. We endeavor to renounce small-mindedness. We use renunciation to glimpse egolessness. Once we have that glimpse, we feel when our ego is trying to cover over those openings or moments of egolessness.

During one week-long sitting, I had a discussion with a participant who was also in recovery that illustrated the need to maintain watchfulness. "Earlier this week I realized that my daily energy drink habit had slowly increased over the last few months, from one a day to more than four, which would have been one thing in and of itself, but I was hiding the fact that I was drinking so many of them from my wife. The hiding is the behavior I needed to renounce." The Warrior must be honest and genuine with ourselves. To do so we must maintain our gentleness. We cannot set out on a rigid regimen of purity and expect immediate results. Typically, change is said to only occur under one impetuous; pain. When we are in enough pain we become ready to change. With time we become more sensitive to that pain. It is said that a realized being feels pain the way we feel an eyelash caught in our eye; they would feel the eyelash in the palm of their hand. We begin at the beginning, and work to renounce those larger behaviors that cause us pain, then we renounce those things that keep us from being open to the world.

Little by little we renounce the stories that we tell ourselves that limit our world and our view of the world. This goes back to the beginning of the chapter--what would happen if we dropped the stories we tell ourselves? Going back even farther, to Chapter 1, we discussed how this one label of being an addict or alcoholic or someone of an addictive nature is something that goes beyond renunciation. We renounce the use of substances to avoid reality. We used those substances to numb ourselves to the world. Anything I use to create a barrier between myself and others is to be rejected. Drinking creates a barrier between me and the world. Defining myself as an alcoholic only creates a barrier between myself and the world if I so let it. The Big Book says that the alcoholic can go anywhere so long as we have business being there. What I need to let go of is the shame and guilt I associated with calling myself an alcoholic.

Every day all over the world people renounce the substance that caused them so much misery. It is that initial act of daring which we repeat every time we introduce ourselves at a meeting or honestly look at ourselves in the mirror. Our proclamation to the world is an act of warriorship.

Once we proclaim our warriorship we also give up our inner world. We endeavor to be of service, to give up our privacy, to live honestly and genuinely. This relates to the concepts within the rooms of recovery of never saying no and never giving up on someone. There are always plenty of opportunities for service work, to help another, both within the rooms and throughout the sangha. We do not need to wait till the twelfth step to begin service work. The world needs us in these dark times. We can help when no one else can. Whenever we want to slink back into the shadows and hide, to indulge our desires for privacy, stability and comfort, we need to resist that urge and step farther into the world. Through many different avenues and methods we are opening up the walls of our fortress. This is not a simple, nor a one-and-done task, resisting our desire for privacy, stability and comfort. We are taking a sledgehammer to that crusty, nasty, spiny stuff that once surrounded our hearts. Sure, it's easier to stay in that shell, but we have tasted something greater than ourselves. Once we have tasted basic goodness we know going backwards is not the way. We give up our privacy. The world is a 24 hour a day, seven day a week call to awakening. We are never not on the spot to respond. Whether it be the hand of AA or an open heart, we proclaim our warriorship.

I am Eric and I am an alcoholic.

The Drala Principle

When we proclaim our warriorship, we begin a journey to experience the world as it truly is. When we do so we discover a sense of dignity and celebration. That sense of dignity begins to uncover a new world, a world that is exactly like the one we were in, but filled with magic. Earlier we discussed how the world we see is not actually as it is. Just one little flower is an incredible proclamation of the entire history of the world. For you to experience that flower is an incredible sense of magic or coincidence. When we are open to the world around us, experiencing it as it truly is, a great ocean of energy is there for us to see. This wisdom and power are known as drala. Drala in Tibetan means "above or beyond the enemy." It is a wisdom beyond aggression. When we relax and are relating with things properly we begin to connect with this power.

There are drala in everything and we can connect with that power. We can also court that power. There are drala of the earth and sky, grass and flowers, the lineage and on and on. When we feel this connection to the world the world responds. If we are slacking off, usually the dralas remind us when we stub our toe, spill a drink or bump into a wall. When we are connected to our own dignity, we feel the dralas around us. They are drawn to our innate power and energy.

The drala principle reminds me of "God's hands" in the rooms of recovery. People make statements like "My higher power brought this person into my life" or made such and such happen. The lights change at just the right time, or a parking spot seems to open up right where you need one. In all the numerous ways that you hear this everyday magic unfolding for people in the rooms, this is connected to the drala principle. Things just seem to happen, or as it is said we experience "auspicious coincidences." The more we build merit and virtue, the more we connect to the natural flow of the world and these magical moments seem to happen.

Basic Sobriety

Even before we get into the real heavy lifting of "cleaning up the wreckage of the past" in steps eight and nine, we have begun preparing for it already. We are planting the seeds for any of the words and deeds that we will enact during our ninth step; we are beginning to bring the ideals and principles into our lives now. We are working to let go of these behaviors that shut us off from the world. Little things start to be put in order around us, little things like making our bed and folding laundry or doing the dishes and sweeping the floor. We are beginning to make our environment welcoming for the dralas. We are starting to create a sense of harmony in the world around us. You know how it feels different after you've cleaned your house or your room? When our desk is neat we seem to work just a little more effectively and we smile more. All of these little tiny pieces of our world start to show how we are relating with our environment properly.

An example from Roger's court battle story: *When I was in the court battle for my son, his mother submitted pictures of my pre-sobriety residence as evidence of my low manner of living. During that time I was drinking and full of self loathing. This manifested in not caring much about my world or my home. One day she came over to use the laundry machine and found the house in a particularly bad, albeit somewhat typical, way. There were dishes piled high and crusty in the sink, toys and clothes everywhere and nothing was put away. The back porch was the usual morning after of beer cans and cigarette butts. This prompted her to call Child Protective Services on me. Now, while I admit that it could have been much worse, it was still pretty bad and not a place that you'd send your child to play for the afternoon or want your two-year-old living. Luckily the dralas were smiling on me for on the day that Child Protective Services did show up I was having some people over for dinner. As a result of getting ready for guests, the place was rather clean and tidy. During the interview with the woman from Child Protective Services, my two-year-old was dumping bins of toys out on the woman's feet looking for a truck. We chatted nicely; I lied and said that this state of cleanliness was typical and I did not understand why my ex was so concerned. Yet, years later, seeing those pictures, even I was disgusted by the low level of cleanliness that I was willing to accept and allow myself and my child to live in.*

Myself I am not the neatest of people, but I cleaned my apartment more times in the first 90 days of sobriety than I had in the previous 3 years. I made my bed each morning. I took showers and shaved regularly. Coming home to my apartment in those early days felt good. I was inviting the dralas into my home and inviting their positive energy, even though I did not know it yet. It felt good and that goodness is the energy of the dralas.

Showering regularly and keeping my body and clothes cleaner began to help me feel better about myself. This invites the dralas to us. As we sit in meditation and connect our head and shoulders, we continue to magnetize the dralas to us. Little by little, any time we find ourselves slipping backwards and taking time off, even within our own bodies, we start to feel a bit grimy. Experiencing a sense of ourselves and a oneness within our own body is the experience of internal drala. The drala energy mixes with our own natural confidence to create further energy, a type of energy we will discuss later, known as windhorse.

When we are in harmony with the world around us, we can feel the energy and that always manifests as a sense of confidence. That confidence is to do what is the appropriate action in any situation. When we care for the world around us, care for ourselves and others, we are inviting the dralas to us. We can all feel the places the dralas have deserted, those ruined landscapes or dingy parts of the city. Yet if we care for those areas, they too can have the dralas return.

No matter how far down the scale we have gone, we too can have the dralas return to our lives.

Step Eight

Made a list of all persons we had harmed and became willing to make amends to them all. (Big Book of AA)

Harm

The 12 and 12 says that at this stage of the game we are "learning how to live in the greatest peace, partnership and brotherhood with all men and women" (Twelve Steps and Twelve Traditions). This is no small order for alcoholics and addicts; for a long time we lived anything but that kind of life. Learning to live in peace with our fellow man, a sense of brotherhood, a partnership with those around us is going to take some work. In many ways this is where the rubber meets the road, as we need to get right with those around us. In the same way we needed to stay present in what we were doing, similar to when we wrote our inventory, without concern for the telling of our inventory to another human being, we need to name those we have harmed without concern with the next step of making amends.

Some may simply pull out their Fourth Step, which will surely have many people whom we have harmed on it, and be done. Yet if we just glibly play lip service to this step, we will be missing a valuable tool in dealing with the world, as well as a valuable piece of our own development. Many will skim over this step because coming to the realization of the harms we have done is an experience many would prefer not to do. When we did the Fourth Step we worked with our resentments, which is different from those we have harmed. Our resentments were generally based on things that were done to us, real or imagined. When we took a deeper look at these resentments we found that we had a part to play in things as well. The other column we discussed earlier, the "sins" or the "stuff I felt bad about" column, held a great many acts of harm that were not necessarily begun by another person. These are the ones I hurt.

Now some may say I did not hurt anyone. I drank by myself, or at the bar; I never hurt anyone but myself. Or there will be the flip side of the coin, the person who believes that if you crossed paths with them, then they did you some harm, because they were such a bad person. In ways, both are right and both are wrong; however, in these two scenarios the person is not seeing the depth of their actions properly. Where we need to fall is somewhere in the middle.

As much as I want to think the period of time I spent drinking on my back porch night after night after night hurt nobody but me, that is simply not true. I surely did not perform well at work on three hours of sleep, probably still drunk from the night before, more concerned with not throwing up on my boss's shoes than on what she was saying. Each night I couldn't wait for my children and wife to fall asleep so I could drink without anyone keeping track of how many I drank, because I deserved to get drunk after such a difficult day (and all days were difficult, no matter what happened in them). When I woke in the morning, on limited sleep, being asked to play that role of Daddy, I was generally not too pleasant.

Interdependence illuminates the fact that no matter what, that my actions never occur in a bubble. Most alcoholics and addicts tended to believe that they lived in a bubble, thinking we were pulling the wool over everyone's eyes, that no one knew how much we were drinking and drugging or when we were in our addiction. As a result we bumbled through many people's lives, justifying and excusing our actions. We never understood why people acted the way they did, but most of the time it was our actions that prompted the way people treated us.

So what we need is to have a working definition of harm, one that we can all agree on. The dictionary defines harm as "physical injury," which probably didn't cover the vast majority of our "harms". It is the synonyms for harm that help us see where we need to look: injure, hurt, wound, misuse, ill-treat, ill-use, abuse, molest. With this expanded definition of harm I may be a little more open to see where I really may have done some damage, because the leveling of pride is in the acceptance of our having done these actions. Many times, we want to say "while in my disease" or "while I was drinking" I did those things, but I would never do them sober. Yet I know most of the time I just did them and used "I was drunk" as a way to not have to admit to myself that I did the things I did. I am sure we all have those things that we wish we didn't do.

The outrageous thing is that we are going to own up to them. Good or bad, I did them. We are all too quick and glad to lay claim to a good behavior or action, and we run like hell away from the bad stuff. The most pain I ever cause myself is when I am not living up to the expectation I set for myself. I should be better than this, I should be pure and saintly, never doing anything that caused the slightest bit of worry or pain to anyone. Yet I've got the last 4 steps showing me all those warts and scars. That is who I am right now, without drugs and alcohol. That person who I was while drinking terrifies me, but I can no longer deny that I am also that person. That person never goes away, especially if I try to hide it away. The more we try to resist that person inside of us, the more it grows. In fact, it grows more ominous by the day. What if my secret got out; what if everyone knew? So the first person we harmed was ourself but not just by our drinking and drugging. We ripped ourselves to shreds internally, externally and every way in between. How much energy do we need to use to keep all that stuff hidden away? How much harm do we continue to do to ourselves keeping that negative energy trapped inside of us? We were internally as destructive as we were externally. Externally we were the center of the bomb blast and from its shockwaves damage emanated.

We need to become aware of the different and varied means by which we hurt those people around us. We can return to the 10 Virtuous and Non-Virtuous Acts to see whom we have treated in these ways. To repeat the Ten Acts of Unmeritorious Karma, they are: taking life, stealing, sexual misconduct, telling lies, causing intrigue, negative words, gossip, envy, hoping to do harm and disbelieving in the truth. By these acts we hurt others to varying degrees.

Further, sometimes when we hurt one person, the effect of that action is felt by many others. When I fought with my wife and she would go stay with her family till things cooled down, this caused numerous worries and inconveniences to her family. Suddenly one single event ripples outward in ever-expanding circles. All we ever saw was the immediate, how it impacted us, effects of an action. We didn't care about the sleepless nights we caused others, the tearful conversations, the scared parents, partners or children.

No Way in Hell Amends

Once we have a list in hand, we can divide the list into a few categories with the help of our sponsor. There are the easy amends to make, there is the group of people whom my ego tells me I harmed but I didn't, there is the group of people to whom making amends would be more harmful than helpful, there is the group of difficult amends and the last group of "No way in hell am I making amends to that S.O.B.". This is the group that we need to work on the most. We need to become willing to make amends to them all. This is the work of Step 8. This is the nitty gritty hard work we must do here to melt the barriers, to open us up to be able to deal with not just the people we love but those that we dislike and hate.

A sponsee had a particular family member on the "no way in hell am I making amends to them" list, a man whom he had not seen in twenty years, but felt much anger and hatred along with guilt and shame over the way things went--his ex-stepfather. He tells this story about the process of dealing those people in the "no way" column.

Our relationship had started well when he first met my mother, while I was young and thoroughly into sports. As I grew older our relationship faded more and more. On my end, beer and girls started to fill the time I once spent playing baseball. The more I began to grow into what I thought was a man, the more we butted heads. My parents made an early attempt to dam the tide of bad behavior by sending me to an all-boys

Basic Sobriety

Catholic high school, because by the time I was finished with eighth grade I had been thrown out of all the honors programs. The initial resentment I had about the all-boys school part was balanced out by the positive of the school having a highly ranked baseball team. I tell all this, because part of our conflict was that I was never up to the level he had me slated to perform at in academics and sports. Oh, I did ok by most people's standards, top 10% of my class, 4-year varsity letter in baseball, captain and MVP my senior year, and when I graduated I had a full semester of college done. Although in hindsight things probably would have been a bit different had I not spent most of my time drinking, planning on drinking, making money to afford drinking and chasing girls.

I hid my drinking pretty well, or so I thought. My stepfather was "leery" of my proclaimed abstinence. He would go to my mother with his concerns and she would not believe him. This caused a major rift between them. In his own struggles in life, he was a brilliant man, an accomplished doctor at a major metropolitan hospital, but completely off his rocker if you asked the sixteen-year-old me. When I turned eighteen our conflicts escalated. Probably unjustly, I truly despised the man by the time I left for college. If it were not for him I could have had a lot more fun in high school, or so I thought at the time, although because of the alcoholic trait of "I'll show him," I had actually accomplished a lot more than if I was left to my own motivational tactics.

The last night before I went off to college, my friends and I had a final celebration which consisted of a bottle of 151 rum and many more substances. Having drunk a large portion of the bottle of 151, my friends left me sick and incoherent at the end of my driveway. They were not going to hang around for me to be discovered in that state. I managed to make it into my bedroom. Unfortunately I threw up in a number of places between the end of the driveway and my room. It was in this condition that my mother found me. I remember her shaking me, trying to figure out what was wrong with me. I know I lied about the amount and type of drinking I had done that evening and promptly threw up again. The gig was up. The four-hour drive the next day to college seemed like an eternity of "How could you?" and "We are so disappointed." Of course the words were wasted on me;

whatever I said to assure them of my desire to not drink again was a complete and utter lie. Once I was settled in my dorm room and my parents gone, I unwrapped a pack of cigarettes and the three bottles of liquor hidden among my belongings and life at school began.

The following year, in what I can only believe was a fit of paranoia, my stepfather left the head of the department at the hospital and signed up for the Air Force. From there I did not see him much. When he signed up for a second tour, my mother filed for divorce. I never saw the man again. My life went on and so did his, but I knew he blamed me for the downfall of his marriage. I could live with the between him and me stuff, but it was because of my mother and half-sister that I felt a constant gnawing in my gut when I thought of him. What my behavior did was cause a rift between him and my mother. During those years after he left our life I would frequently reflect on him. "Oh yeah, my lying caused a lot of harm BUT..." I had a list as long as my arm about what an asshole he was to me, my siblings and my mother so FUCK HIM, no way in hell I am making amends for that.

This is where the Eighth Step, "became willing," came into play. Behind the bravado of all his harms to me was a huge amount of guilt. I have found the worst guilt came when my actions created ripples of destruction. Seventeen-year-old kid getting drunk is par for the course. Seventeen-year-old kid creating enough sand in the ointment to cause a marriage to fail, causing my half-sister to live without a father figure, my mother's misery-- well, that kind of stuck with me through the years. The problem was that without the alcohol to silence the guilt, it was there like a festering wound, getting worse as I continued to clean up the other messes in my life. It was pretty painful. A friend described it as a twenty pound sack of shit I was carrying around with me everywhere I went, and that if I wanted to be relieved of the sack, all I needed to was "become willing to make amends to them all." So after much praying and discussion with others, the pain made me willing to open my heart. For weeks I would pray, work loving-kindness, and work my own guilt till one day I reached a state of willingness.

The Eighth Step was where the magic began to happen for me. The more I became willing to own my part in the troubles, to let go of the wrongs done me, the more I started to experience peace.

Basic Sobriety

Tonglen and Compassion

Within the Buddhadharma, one of the primary practices for building compassion for others is through tonglen. Tonglen is the practice of giving and taking, or sending and receiving. The practice of tonglen is described well in Shantideva's[15] Way of the Bodhisattva.

Whatever joy there is in this world
All comes from desiring others to be happy,
And whatever suffering there is in this world
All comes from desiring myself to be happy.
If I do not actually exchange my happiness
For the sufferings of others,
I shall not attain the state of Buddhahood
And even in cyclic existence I shall have no joy.

It was later transmitted to the Tibetans by Atisha[16]. Atisha's method of tonglen was further taught through the Lojong (or mind-training) slogans.

Sending and taking should be practiced alternately. These two should ride the breath.

The practice of tonglen is seen as an important practice for working with the boundary between self and other, as well as developing compassion for others by developing the willingness to take on their pain and suffering. Notice the word willingness. It goes

---

[15] Shantideva was an 8th century Indian Buddhist monk and scholar. The Way of the Bodhisattva or Bodhicaryavatara is a description of the process of enlightenment from first crude thought to Buddhahood.

[16] 11th century Bengali Buddhist monk who was influential in the spread of Buddhism throughout Tibet.

completely against our societal instincts of resisting that which is bad and coveting only that which is good.

In the practice of tonglen we flip the current, and we take in that which is bad and send out that which is good. We can do this on many levels and under different circumstances. Usually when we think of this concept, the typical reaction is "Why the hell do I want to take on people's pain? I have enough crap of my own to deal with." Valid point, which is about where we felt we were when we started writing down step eight. There were some people who we were very willing to be making amends to and others who were in that "no way in hell" category. AA has been utilizing this practice in two forms for decades: group sharing and working with another alcoholic. If nothing assures my own sobriety like working with someone who is in pain, then the question is why? I can't get another person sober and I cannot get them drunk. So what am I doing? In its simplest form, we are directly working with tonglen. In early sobriety or at any time, for that matter, when you get hooked by something and you freak out, AA tells you to do two things: 1) share it with another alcoholic or 2) take it to a meeting. In both cases the same thing happens, you send your bad and receive their good. They take your crazy and breathe into you their calm.

This is one of the beauties of the twelve step community that differs from most societal dynamics. Acharya Fleet Maul describes the typical societal interaction as a "drama triangle." Good guy, bad guy, and the victim are the three points of the triangle. In every situation we generally interact from one of those three positions. Generally the victim is hurt by the bad guy, so the victim looks to the good guy for validation and support. In most cases when the victim calls up the good guy, they are looking for the good guy to back their position--"Can you believe what John did to me?"--and the good guy says right on cue, "Oh my, I can't believe he did that to you" and the two of you go building a case against the bad guy. Through the fourth and fifth steps, AA doesn't like the victim mentality; we focus on our part of every situation. When you make that phone call to kvetch about John, you generally don't get that "poor baby" response. What typically happens is you call your sponsor (or any other person in recovery) all freaked out about a situation, full of negative energy, ranting and fuming. They take in your crazy, because they don't go into "good guy" mode. They listen and breathe out calm to you. They give some advice based on their experience and we are "relieved" of the negative energy. The person took on our bad energy and gave us some of their good energy. Taking on this energy didn't make them explode. They could handle the energy because of their own reserve of strength and experience. This happens in the groups as well. Someone comes in with a problem and we all breathe in the bad energy and try to give our peaceful, good energy in return by sharing our experience, strength and hope.

Taking the idea of tonglen out of the realm of the esoteric and into the everyday life shows how we are already familiar with the form. Each time we freak out and receive some peace in return, we are building our own strength to do this for others in turn. Little by little the things that once caused major turmoil slowly begin to change into less and less of a reaction, or at least an appropriate reaction. Just as the sunlight is brilliant and painful when we first take off our sunglasses, our eyes slowly adjust. The intensity of the sun has not changed but our ability to handle the intensity has changed. This is how tonglen works within us or how tonglen grows our ability to experience the world.

There are formal and informal ways of doing tonglen. Honestly, for myself sometimes the formal way can be difficult to do. In the more formal practice, you first sit in meditation to rest your mind, then you bring to mind someone you love or someone close to you in pain, basically something to help open the heart. Then you breathe in their hot pain and breathe out your cool healing serenity. As you get comfortable you increase your range of people whose pain you are breathing in and whom you are sending the cool calm good air to, until you cover the entire universe.

In the Moment Tonglen

What I have found is that I have been able to use tonglen as a practical everyday tool to help work with powerful emotions and not become overwhelmed by them by connect with the greater world. Using tonglen we can not only exchange the good and bad, or bad for good, but we can completely exchange self for other. We know that the people who are on our list have a great deal of hurt and anger because of our actions. Working tonglen in this situation helps us to become willing to sit in those emotional fires and know we will not be burned.

When we are completely hooked by an emotion, and we are aware of it, we need a way to dissipate the energy of the emotion. It is in these moments that I have found tonglen to be extremely practical. Step Eight is about the principle of brotherhood with mankind; it is our shared humanity with all mankind that tonglen helps us to connect with. At any moment we can be in a situation that hooks us, whether it is a big situation like the death of a parent or a small one like the boss wanting to ask a question. When we have the awareness to know that we are completely hooked, we can take a breath and locate what we are feeling. When we do this we can look deeper to see both the story and the emotion. They are entwined but separate, like threads in a rope. "I am nervous" and "because the boss wants to ask me something" are the cause and condition of the moment. What I am feeling is "real" in the moment and the stuff about the boss is the basis for story that I'm blowing all out of proportion. Allowing yourself to feel the emotion will allow it to rise and fall away. It will have a beginning, middle and an end, if we stop the story. It's when we get wrapped up in the story that causes us to spin off out of control.

The on-the-spot tonglen practice I work with is, "This is what someone feels when _____." This first allows the emotions to exist without resistance or shame. Emotions are natural and I need to remind myself that it is ok to feel. Resistance breeds persistence so I need to let the emotion free to be felt. Then I take a breath in,

Basic Sobriety

thinking that others too feel this way in the same situation. There are 7 billion people in the world and chances are at that very moment, others are going through the same emotion. I am not alone in how I feel, so I can use this shared humanity of the emotion to connect myself to all those others, each breath reaching people farther and farther out from myself. There is a realization that occurs that I can hold my own emotion without exploding or dying. Then the thought comes, *Wouldn't it be great if some other people's emotions could be relieved?* So with each breath, knowing I can hold my own anxiety (as an example), I take on a little of their anxiety on the in-breath and exhale some calm and peace. Sure enough, my own anxiety fades away as my compassion for others grows in the moment. The nice calm breathing doesn't hurt either.

Most importantly, to the alcoholic addict, this connection in the moment erases the "why is this happening to ME" question. Expanding my awareness gives my own emotions space. Thinking of others who may be going through the same emotion connects me to the brotherhood of man. No longer is it that I am under attack by the situation. The situation is no longer pinpointing me; I am just one among many, "a worker among workers," who happens to be dealing with desire, death, divorce or despair (or whatever it may be), the same as all those other people. I am not so unique. The more I connect with the feeling of it not being about me, the more I can connect with others during the process. In the end the negative energy is transmuted into positive energy.

The next style of tonglen occurs spontaneously during a meditation session, when something keeps coming up instead of quickly labeling it thinking for the tenth time and pushing it away (notice I didn't say letting go). Hopefully, you can relate to sitting there and as much as you'd rather not be worrying about the doctor's appointment next week or about what is going to happen at the meeting later in the day, you just keep returning again over and over to the thought. The thoughts spur emotions and we are hooked. So even though our intent when we sat down was not to do a tonglen session, I have found that it is at these times that working with tonglen is very helpful. When I first find myself caught by a strong emotion, it may be a one-off feeling and so just separating the storyline from the emotion may be enough for it to rise and fall away. However, there are times when it continues to arise. When it seems that I cannot "let go" of the persistent thought / story / emotion something else needs to be done. Instead of trying to deny and push it away, it is better to accept that this is where I am at in that moment and best to work with it. At that point using the persistent emotion first within myself and then to connect with others and the world allows for the emotion to become workable, turning the negative emotion to a positive use.

Exchanging Self For Others

The effect of exchanging our self for others is that it begins to stabilize our emotional state. The more we connect to those around us, the more we see that they are same as we are, going through the same difficult emotions, the more we equalize our self-image. Not only do we see that our troubles are not completely unique to ME, who so wants everything to be about me, but that everyone else feels exactly the way we do at some time or another. The beauty of this is that we don't have to get drunk or use over whatever we may be feeling.

If we continue with the thought of exchanging self for other, we see that we have only been taking and giving part of ourselves. When you are sitting there breathing in the fear of a friend who is going through a tough period, you may say to yourself, "The fear is fine, but that crazy over there in her life, I ain't touching!" or conversely, "Here is some peace and calm with regard to your sickness but you don't need the insanity I got brewing over here." We cannot be picky about what we give and take. We have to exchange all of us for all of them. This is a very powerful proposition. This idea of sending all of our self and taking all of them feels like one of those situational comedies where the mother and daughter exchange souls during the night, waking up in the other's body.

What good can possibly come of this? I send all my bad memories, feelings of guilt and shame over to some unsuspecting person? I've seen their crazy and I don't want it! In fact, it was that resistance that showed me exactly what I was working with. A friend once told me that if all of us in the room put all our problems on the table and then were asked to take any problems back, generally we would take our own problems back. As much as they are "problems," they are our problems and we know them well. The idea of really taking on others' problems, even at this spiritual level, can be very difficult to overcome, or so it seems. The more I have sat with this style of tonglen, fully taking and sending, the hazier the ideas of good and bad become. We looked at all of our character defects and shortcomings in Steps Six and Seven, so we know there is no black and white, clear-cut line here. Also, looking back at the earlier steps, I know that all of these pieces and parts, these stories and shortcomings are not who we fundamentally are. Sure, they have manifested in all sorts of neuroses but they are not fundamentally who we are.

So what are we sending and receiving? What we are working with is the fundamental state of who we are and who everyone is. Maybe you want to describe it as--energy, light, goodness, or a soul. What I found for myself is that when all of the stories fall away, there has never been nor ever will be a stain on my "soul". There are moments I forget this and there are moments that I know this. When I drop all the stories I see everything within myself as worthy of being given away, and I can give it all away. When I drop all the stories about myself, then I drop the stories about the other person, and I can see that there are no stains on their soul either. Continuously breaking down the boundary between self and other develops love and compassion for others and from there we become willing to let go and forgive. When the resistance falls away, what are we left with? Nothing but a willingness to make amends to them all.

Outrageous Willingness

Tonglen works to open our heart and develop bodhicitta, an awakened heart. This is pretty crazy stuff in that we are continually pushing the boundary of our comfort zones. We are continuing the path of outrageousness. It is ironic that the dictionary gives one definition of outrageous as being "shockingly bad or excessive," which is how we felt we behaved and acted during our addiction, and a second definition is being "very bold, unusual and startling," which is exactly what setting out on a path of amends is. Looking deeper outrageousness has been described as having five categories or qualities: fearlessness, cheerfulness, gentleness, daring and synchronizing mind and body.

In many ways we have already been working with these qualities. The willingness to face our fears and approach people we have harmed is an act of fearlessness. We have run from these fears for long enough. We do not have to delude ourselves into thinking that everything will be all "it's ok" and "never mind," but whatever is going to happen we will in fact be ok. This is the outrageous aspect of fearlessness. We don't have to fight with the fears; we don't need to push anything aside; we can just walk through them. Whatever is going to happen is going to happen; we know that the universe will provide us with a response. It is those gray area people—the ones that we don't know if they will slam the door in our face, punch us in the nose or hug us--that cause the most fear. The warriorship of outrageous acknowledges the fear and goes for it anyway.

We've discussed doubt and hope in the previous steps, so we have that open space to step into when we are preparing to make amends. When we are without a sense of fear about what is about to happen, we can be cheerful about what we are about to do. One way or the other we will get a response and we will be open and present to it, and that has a sense of cheerfulness to it. Years of fearing something will be over once we are on the other side of the amends, so we perk up. Since we are free of the hope and fear, and we have been working with our open heart, we know to be gentle with ourselves. Gentleness in looking backward at the acts that caused the harm. Gentleness looking forward in knowing we have become willing to let go of the ages-old hate and fear. Gentleness because we know that there is nothing but goodness inside ourselves and those we harmed. We know we are not going to these people to wage war but to end the wars.

All of these qualities together create daring. The willingness to go to these people after sometimes decades of hatred is a completely daring act. We've heard that doing this will be good for us, but we have to experience it for ourselves. This sets us up for going forward into step nine. Adding that sense of daring to our fearlessness, cheerfulness, and gentleness creates a sense of dignity and refinement within us. Like a noble knight, a warrior without armor, a warrior without fear, our body and mind are synchronized. At this point we have spent a lot of time getting to know our inner world, that connection between our mind and body. Upliftedness is not arrogance--we still know the harms we have done--but we are no longer weighed down by our past. This moment is good. Having done a lot of work and inventory, character defects and shortcomings all come together with a sense of purpose. Without even having to think about it, our head is high and our shoulders back; we have synchronized our mind and body.

With that we are ready for the next step of our journey.

Step Nine

Made direct amends to such people wherever possible, except when to do so would injure them or others. (Big Book of AA)

For every ounce of fear I had going into this Step, the reward was a hundredfold release and relief. This was where I began to truly feel the "new freedom and a new happiness" that the ninth step promises. The problem was that I kept hearing these promises, day after day, since I got sober, and I wanted them right then. While doing the Ninth Step, somewhere along the way everything changed.

A Lying Child

Tonight I had to have a talk with my youngest daughter about lying. She had gotten into minor trouble during school and the result was a yellow day. The yellow day by itself is not such a big thing, as we all have a bad day every now and then. If I can excuse myself for having a bad day, more of them than I would like to admit, surely I can excuse her for having a bad day. What made the matter pressing was that she first tried to pin the reason for her behavior on someone else and skipped that her teacher had to speak to her numerous times today. When the time was appropriate to discuss the two issues, we discussed taking responsibility for our own actions and how to tell the "bad thing" first. During our discussion she said, "Dad, I wish I knew when I started lying so I can go back and see why I started this habit of lying." Not bad for a seven-year-old.

However, it's not about going back to that first lie, whether it was yesterday or years ago, but about knowing why we are doing it now and how we can go forward from here--in other words, amending our behavior. We can go back to that story of the poison arrow and want to know who shot it, what they had for lunch and who made the arrow, or we can remove the arrow. I am going to guess her reason for lying was the same as mine when I would lie to my parents many years ago, for in my mind I created a punishment that I didn't want to experience. Back then, and even today, lying was not about wanting to deceive you just to deceive you; I lied in the attempt to protect myself from the punishment I had imagined. I hoped to say the things that would keep me out of trouble. Unfortunately, I inevitably got caught in the lie and thus I was punished even more harshly. The result was that I got to experience the punishment I had conjured in my mind, and having hated having to experience that punishment, tried to do better with my lies the next time. I had no intention of being honest before sobriety. All I endeavored to do was tell better lies, to tell craftier and more believable lies. Similar to our addiction, we begin from a point of trying to protect ourselves and in the end continue to do more and greater harm.

Justice

In its simplest form much of my discussion with my daughter lays the groundwork for the ninth step. We are going to take responsibility for our actions and go right into the "bad stuff," then we are going to amend our behavior (or right wrongs where possible). The problem is how? The Twelve and Twelve devotes a scant five pages to it, giving two very pithy instructions: "Good judgment, a careful sense of timing, courage and prudence - these are the qualities we shall need when we take Step Nine" and "we must be sure to remember that we cannot buy our own peace of mind at the expense of others." The Big Book reminds us of how important this step is, but does not get much into why or how. Returning to those pithy instructions from the Twelve and Twelve, we may compare "a careful sense of timing, courage and prudence" to the concept of "skillful means," which is also called upaya in Sanskrit, as well as another very Buddhist concept of "don't make things worse."

So with our list in hand, first we need to review the list with our sponsor. That is a great rule of thumb. Who we feel we need to make amends to may not be who we should make amends to. Worse, our motive for making amends to some people has nothing to do with actually making amends. We need to be sure that our motives are what they need to be or we will be making matters worse, never better. It is also a good habit to review with your sponsor what you are going to say and what you are going to not say. This is where the idea of Right Speech definitely comes into play. Remember we cannot save our ass at the expense of another, so it can be very beneficial to go over what you are going to say, or have your sponsor review any written materials before sending. Some sponsors even do a little bit of role playing, so you can get comfortable with the words coming out of your mouth and how you might react if the conversation does not go according to your plan.

It is interesting that the Twelve Step principle that this step represents is "justice." When it has served our purposes many of us have held a very strict sense of justice. Unfortunately, it seemed that most of the time we felt that we were in the right and everyone else was in the wrong. When it came to the behaviors of others, there was not much gray area. When it came to our own actions and behaviors, well, there was a lot of room to swim in that gray area. Much of my own idea of justice was based on a very arcane sense of right and wrong, and more specifically punishment and damnation. Our society helps to manifest these ideas by the judicial and legal systems. Frequently our governmental elements make laws that appear to be based on someone's idea of morality rather than some universal truth.

My own sense of universal truths continually had me raging against people and loved ones. *Don't you know that you fold the laundry this way and that the green coffee cup must always be placed on the third shelf* were universal truths that I felt all people should intrinsically know. Watch yourself while driving or at the grocery store and you will soon realize you may hold a number of these truths to be "self-evident" to no one but yourself. Unfortunately, frequently the result of someone breaking these rules meant that they needed to be punished. It was taken to a whole new level when someone needed to be punished because they hurt me. Eye for an eye was the code in the old days, but usually it was more like an arm for a little finger. Justice was more likely served vigilante or guerilla style. I may have bounced yet another check, so to balance the scale of my own feeling bad, I needed to treat you poorly until you felt as bad as or worse than I did for reprimanding me about not being more careful with the household money. Not a very true sense of justice, is it?

So what is justice? Justice can be defined as "just behavior or treatment". How am I to behave? The definition of just is "based on or behaving according to what is morally right and fair." Ok, this is getting a bit closer to what may work, but morality can be an issue as we have seen in the Fourth Step. Here in the Ninth Step let's look at the definition of moral: "of, relating to, or concerned with the principles or rule of right conduct or the distinction between right and wrong, ethical." Subsequent definitions continue to repeat one phrase over and over again: right conduct. In fact, it is not until you look further down the different definitions of justice that you see anything about reward and punishment. What we are looking to do is treat people properly, to have right conduct toward ourselves and others. That seems pretty doable. Unfortunately, our past conduct wasn't so "right." In fact, our past conduct was usually completely wrapped up in passion, aggression and ignorance, such that our conduct was less than ethical and ran counter to those around us. In essence we were so wrapped up in our own little schemes of the "me plan" that we didn't give much regard to anyone unless it could benefit us.

Damaged Relationships

Sadly, my first wife and I did not divorce under amicable conditions. We would argue for days and weeks over trivial issues. Neither of us was able to give an inch and we were both willing to bite our own noses off to spite our faces. My drinking, ferocious resentment to the situation and uncontrolled anger did nothing to calm the waters between us. Our inability to be in the same room together without the anger being palpable made our two daughters very uneasy. I was particularly biting to the new man who had entered her life.

What I discovered in the process of the steps was that what I originally thought about why we got divorced was not the truth. I could never understand why we would rub each other the wrong way so often. Sure, we were young and pretty foolish, but I could not see the connection between how the fights were the effect and I was the cause. Most days, if we weren't doing what I wanted to do, I was not a happy camper, which resulted in me ruining many an evening. I didn't like her friends because I felt threatened by them. I was manic about trying to please her at times to make up for the times when I was basically an idiot. When I really looked at my relationship with this woman in the Fourth Step, suddenly all the letters she had written that said I was "selfish and self-centered" a dozen years ago actually made sense.

Knowing that I was a major cause of the marriage collapsing helped me to forgive the wrongs I laid on her side of the street. Out of the blue, she didn't just wake up one morning and say, "I'm done". It had been coming for some time. The closer we got to our marriage falling apart, the more I was drinking, which only exacerbated matters. I was blaming my unhappiness on her. When she first mentioned I had a drinking problem, I tried to control my drinking. Not having a few drinks after work each night resulted in weekend binges, which she chose not to be around anymore. In the end we lived on separate floors of the house when we were there together, and on weekends we started alternating who got to be at home with the kids. I tried therapy at one point, but only to confirm that I was not crazy, therefore cementing in my mind that she was the crazy one. Toward the end, I can recall hearing the word "alcoholic" more than once.

Basic Sobriety

After she left, as I said, it was not pleasant. Being left alone in our house without the kids, my drinking really started to kick up. Calling into work became more the norm than the exception. I missed plane flights and morning meetings. Of course, it was living in the house alone that was the problem, so a friend offered to sublet his studio apartment to me. New digs only meant new patterns of the same old habits. Every day I stopped at the little store a few doors down before another night spent drinking, painting, downloading music and watching bad movies, and sleeping little. The first six-pack did not even need to go into the fridge it would be drunk so quickly. The rest of the night would be spent drinking enough to pass out. I rarely went out. In the beginning when my daughters came to visit me, I would stay sober for those few days. Then the drinking started after they went to bed, then when we got home on days I had them. Eventually it did not matter anymore; I drank every day.

Needless to say the next five years slowly progressed in a downward spiral. Wife number two and I fought nearly as much as I fought with wife number one. The drinking became constant when I was not at the office. Then came getting laid off, to my shock and surprise. When the money ran out, with what little we had, we made the decision to move away. The last time I saw wife number one was when I said goodbye to our two daughters, now 6 and 8. That was a cordial exchange, compared to a few days earlier when she took the kids from me in the middle of the day because I was drunk.

Luckily wife number one and those two daughters missed that final year and half of drinking. Wife number two stayed around for another few months before she could no longer handle the drinking, the pity party, the anger and the depression.

Fast forward a number of years, to a recent visit to NY. My oldest daughter was not feeling well. While she lay sick in bed, I spent the next few hours hanging with wife number one's husband, that same guy I once yelled at and hated, in their house while wife number one was taking my daughter from the second marriage and her daughter from her second marriage on a play date. How did it get to this? Step nine. Wife number one was among the first people I needed to make amends to. To do that, I needed to have a little bit of sobriety under my belt so that she knew I was serious. I needed to be showing her that while I still had a way to go with the character defects that made me such an ass to be married to, that those character defects were slowly fading away. Last, I needed to own my part in what had happened. When I told her that I could now honestly see how selfish and self-centered I had truly been, the tears started flowing down her cheeks. Years of feuding faded away. Then I made amends to her husband; having forgiven him for "stealing her away" I was able to let go of the anger and accept that he was a good man and a good stepfather.

Listening

How many have we hurt with our words? Words said in anger, words said in ignorance, words said with ulterior motives--all cause harm. Unlike an action, many times the impact and the ripple effect of a word is not felt immediately. Words spoken can lie within our memories for decades. Meaningless words to one mean so much to someone else. Letters of love, letters of hate and anger, emails, texts, Facebook, Twitter and who knows what--words upon words floating around out there. If only the nursery rhyme were true: "Sticks and stones will break my bones, but words will never harm me."

Step One was all about getting honest with ourselves. Here in Step Nine we are getting honest with others. The importance of this cannot be overlooked. One person honestly talking to another is the foundation for good society. Unfortunately, two people who are deceitful and scheming result in distrust and dark results, which we see all around us in today's "dog eat dog" world, where we all think if we don't lie, cheat and steal to get what we want then someone else will take it from us. The problem is everyone is sitting around the table thinking the same thing: *If I don't then they will.* The result is a society of distrust. The way to build a society of trust is with honesty. When two people are honest with each other, wonderful and marvelous things are possible. This is the root of good society. Our own willingness to be honest with another has the power to open another person up.

Within all the different styles and elements of speech, whether it be sarcasm or slander, lies or barbed truths, the pithy instruction the Buddha teaches that you will also hear paraphrased in the rooms is: "Is it true?" and "Is it useful?" One should say "fire is hot" not "fire seems hot." We speak what is true and what is useful. Much of the time we, and others around us, fill the air with words. Even if it is true that it is a nice day and that in 1985 the Mets brought in a relief pitcher who blew the game, sometimes the guy next to you in the elevator does not need to know that. More importantly, when we are making our amends there will be many items that are true that will not be useful at this time. The Big Book covers this within the step by saying "except when to do so could injure them or others." When we are discussing our past mistakes and errors it is not necessary, nor recommended, to bring every tidbit back into the light. It is important that we stick with our intention to right past wrongs, so we need to be very mindful of the words we use because we do not want to make matters worse or reopen old wounds.

It is more the underlying reasons for our behavior than the behaviors themselves that we address during the amends process. Taking responsibility for our actions and the true reasons why we acted the way we did is a lot more worthwhile than bringing up the laundry list of mistakes we may have made. Since we worked with those underlying reasons, i.e., our shortcomings and character defects, we are in a position to honestly and truly say that we are trying to change. When we are in these situations it is beneficial to remember the six points of mindful speech: speak slowly, enunciate clearly, be concise, listen to yourself, listen to others, and use silence as a part of speech. Sometimes it is just better to say nothing at all.

Listening to others is one aspect that the Big Book does not address during the amends process. Listening is a powerful tool. We can listen someone into their own wisdom. We can be there for someone while they explore ideas and concepts. Listening is a valuable part of the amends process on two levels. When we listen we allow the space for the pains and hurts we caused to be aired. We do not have to react. We do not have to defend. We need to keep our heart open and hear what the other person has to say. We let them express themselves fully, to cleanse their pain and hurt. We bear witness to the wrongs we have done.

The second aspect of listening is we need to find out how we hurt the people in our life. A friend described his lesson of listening to me once; *One Valentine's Day the gift I ordered did not come on time, and the result was that my wife was hurt and upset that I barely acknowledged the day. When we talked about it she said she "did not feel loved and respected." I was a little taken aback; even though the gift was late I thought it was a well-intended and thoughtful gift, I tell her I love her frequently and buy flowers every now and then, etc. So I asked her what "love and respect" looked like to her. This was the valuable lesson; it was not flowers and nice dates, or any of the things under my definition of showing love and respect. Love and respect to her looked like helping out more around the house, picking up my stuff, and helping with the dishes. Here I thought she was upset about the gift, but really there was a deeper feeling of not feeling loved and respected. Without listening I would never have come across those items as her definition of love and respect.*

During the amends process we are not going with our hat in hand to say "I'm sorry". When we say "I'm sorry," we are still holding the power in that they can accept it or not, but it is us who had to make the offer of the apology. That is not what we are doing here. Also, when I say "I'm sorry" it is for the things I think I know about why you are upset. I think I know what I did wrong to you. I do not know what I did to hurt some people, even those closest to me like the above-mentioned example of love and respect. When we ask others how our behaviors made them feel, we are no longer just saying "I'm sorry" the way we did a thousand times before. We have already done our own forgiving in Step Eight, so Step Nine is about them. When we ask how we hurt someone, then we can ask them for forgiveness. When we receive that forgiveness we are truly free. It may be that we have to come back with another means to make the amends once we know where the hurt really lay. It is only through the power of listening that we can fully allow the process to work. Both parties are set free.

Upaya - "Skillful Means"

Through much of my life I searched for the "right action" playbook. You know, the one that everyone else seemed to have. Obviously they knew something that I did not know, because they seemed to handle life so well. Ex-wife is on the phone angry, a diaper needs to be changed, dinner needs to be cooked and I had a shitty day. I wanted the magic genie to appear with a play chart, all the x's and o's diagrammed. Chances were most of the time I ended up calling an audible, or rather an inaudible "f- it, I need a drink." For a long time into sobriety I still found that I was searching for the rule book. If A happens do B. If X happens do Y. I was still looking for the antidotes to each of the poisons of life. I sniffle and take a decongestant, then I ache so I take an aspirin. I was always on the lookout for a set of guidelines that illustrated the "proper way" to handle each and every situation.

In the Buddhist tradition this ability to handle a situation is described as "upaya," or skillful means. Apparently even within Buddhism some of his disciples and students wanted the playbook as well. There became schools of thought that rigorously held to a very strict set of teachings and path to reach enlightenment. No matter who you were, what type of environment you were raised in or the ability you had, if you did these particular practices and thought in this particular way then you would reach enlightenment. On the surface this is great; we have a path all laid out for us to enlightenment. All we have to do is x, y, z and hello enlightenment.

Maybe it works for a few, but not all. Those who do not quite get it all are left scratching their heads, wondering what they did wrong.

Even though the Buddha in essence taught the same thing throughout his life, he did not teach the same thing the same way over and over again. He spent the remainder of his life helping different people of different abilities to achieve enlightenment in many different ways. One size does not fit all. Not only do you have to know the method, but you have to know the audience and the space in which the teachings are given. In some of the teachings, the sutras begin by stating that those of certain abilities will be liberated upon hearing, while others may need to hear it a few times before being liberated, while still others will not be liberated but they will be a little bit closer for the next life.

The Buddha's discourses and stories are full of examples of how various skillful means were utilized to help people achieve liberation. His teachings changed and grew, while still fundamentally focusing on the same ideas. In the beginning it was about one person being liberated. In time, no longer was it just about one person being liberated; it became about all people being liberated. In the Buddha's later teachings lay the idea that liberation could be achieved in a single lifetime. Reading the history of some of the greatest teachers in Tibet's history you find many "interesting" methods used to help someone achieve liberation and enlightenment. In essence the teacher or guru would use unconventional methods to shock their students out of fixed psychological patterns. The teachers, while using these seemingly unconventional methods, were utilizing skillful means to transmit and liberate the student. To teach in this way was called "crazy wisdom."

Working with Negative Energy

Many of the Kagyu teachers throughout history were so-called crazy wisdom teachers. Crazy wisdom refers to a form of wisdom that is unlimited and unconditioned by cultural norms or conventions. It expresses wisdom that is direct and immediate, seeking to be as close to reality as possible. Choygam Trungpa was a crazy wisdom teacher. It was the result of his openness and awareness to what was truly happening or not happening that allowed him to touch his students and those around him in a direct way and sometimes unconventional way. Not having studied directly from the man, I sadly cannot attest to this on a personal level. For our purposes here, it is this idea of crazy wisdom, of being able to work purely with the energy of the moment, that may manifest in unconventional responses. Trungpa leaped into those responses without hesitation because they were the right thing to do for someone, not always the polite or socially correct thing to do. Not only did he leap into that space of unconditional unknowns, but this infused much of his teachings, never allowing the ego to get comfortable enough to start to rebuild its fortress.

Leaping into the unknown, constantly pulling the rug from beneath our belief system is at the core of the Buddha's teachings. We are learning to work with the immediate energy of each moment. The process of the steps of recovery has been helping us to step into that unknown space, i.e., "old ideas availed us nothing." We have been continually looking at the idea of what if I "let this go." Each time we gave up that hallowed ground in our psyche, the result was more freedom, another chain of bondage broken.

We need to work directly with the world, to have strong personal relationships, to be active members of society. The ninth step is that training ground. We have prepared and we have practiced, but nothing is like real situations and so we step into the fear of what may happen during an amend. In working with energy, particularly negative energy, we can look to the Mahakala, mentioned in the first chapter, on how to dispel the confusion and manic energy of others' emotions. The Mahakala has four arms, for four actions or karmayogas which are used to pacify, enrich, magnetize and destroy the neuroses of another--or ourselves, for that matter.

Working with the negative emotions of ourselves and others is the path of the ninth step. The ground of this is that all energies are workable, therefore we can transmute these confused, aggressive and negative energies. These energies can be transmuted or changed from confusion and aggression into wisdom and intelligence. To begin with, we must remain neutral to the energies. We are not able to help anyone once we are hooked ourselves. What is said by the other party is their truth and may not be how we remember things. When our defenses go up we are no longer open to hearing what the other person has to say. Of course, if the other person becomes belligerent or threatening at any point, it may be necessary to leave the situation. Remember, we are not out to cause harm, even to ourselves. There is no guide or rule of thumb, but once we are hooked by our own fear or anger we are no longer able to be open to what is happening and it may be best to return at a later time.

The Mahakala is said to have a tool in each of his four hands with which to transmute negative energy into wisdom. In his first right hand he holds a skull cap filled with calming medicine to pacify and resolve conflicts peacefully. We start by calming ourselves, letting go of the idea of winning or losing, turning our anxiety into curiosity about what the other person is saying. Through listening, asking questions and appreciating what the other person has to say we are seeking to pacify the harm done. In his first left hand he holds a hooked knife which enriches the energy. When our natural tendency to draw up our defenses or to protect our own territory arises the knife cuts through those tendencies and draws to it enriching activities. These enriching activities may be proposing new solutions, offering assistance, making concessions and building mutual respect. Instead of trying to tear down the other person we endeavor to build them up. In the Mahakala's second right hand is a sword which magnetizes abilities and resources. Once we are willing to let go of our territory, we can search for new options and new alternatives. Magnetizing is about making compromises. We come together on a topic, each of us giving a little to resolve the conflict.

Destroying is symbolized by a trident, held in the Mahakala's second left hand. This is what may be necessary if pacifying, enriching and magnetizing do not remedy the situation. It is only because we have been open enough to try those previous methods that this act of destroying is not in anger or frustration. Within the meditation posture it may be said that we have a strong back and a soft heart. We have been open and willing to make our amends, to deal with the situation directly and honestly. Unfortunately we sometimes have to firmly say "no." We are not here to degrade ourselves or to be doormats. We are here to make positive changes. We have been willing to calmly discuss the issues and listen, to propose solutions and even make concessions. Being willing to do all of those things and still no resolution is in sight; sometimes a firm "no" is the only option remaining.

True Compassion

As much as we have been willing to let go, the other person must be willing to forgive as well. This may not always happen. Many will be happy that we are going through this process of recovery, but there will be some who are not ready yet. We can always return again to try at a later time. While some postulate that it is only our responsibility to make the apology and what the other person does with it is up to them, that you have done your part by being willing to make the apology and can now wipe your hands clean of the matter. Others state that we ask for forgiveness, that this is what we humbly ask for and they can bestow on us. Having said "I'm sorry" a thousand times before with little heart, asking for forgiveness is a more humbling and less ego-ridden proposition.

Letting bygones be bygones does not mean that we go skipping off into the sunset hand in hand. Yes, some relationships will be mended, while others will just bury the hatchet. For still others we will "clean our side of the street" and we will let them into our heart but we do not have to let them into our house. Our attempts to turn our lives around and make good do not need to put us into positions where harm may come to us or those around us. We need to have compassion for those around us, but we do not need to have "idiot compassion." Many people in their idea of "living amends" allow things to happen which are not proper or right, excusing their own enabling or lack of boundaries because of all the harms they did in the past. It can be difficult at times with people we love to set those clear boundaries.

Sometimes the most compassionate thing that we can do is to say "No!" Our compassion and equanimity for ourselves comes first. From there we can share it with the world. Idiot compassion lacks intelligence, mistakenly thinking that our actions or lack of actions will not hurt the other person or ourselves. That is the thinking and scheming that we uncovered in our fourth step--the actions done so that people would like us or give us what we wanted. True compassion is honest and for the benefit of all involved. This is the compassionate heart of crazy wisdom. This is the ninth step promise of "We will intuitively know how to handle situations which used to baffle us."

Letting Go

The Garuda is always playing in the open space of possibilities. The Garuda was born in the open space and never touches the earth. The warriors of Garuda have tremendous mercy for others. They provide whatever is needed in any situation. When we provide the open space for anything to happen, we can react appropriately to any situation, applying one of the four karmayogas described above. When we approach with a fixed and rigid mind we are trying to solidify the situation into something that it is not. Yet we are also not merely acting on instinct and reflex, lacking awareness and wisdom. The warrior of Garuda works within the reality of a situation.

Learning to let go, to exist in that open space of the Garuda is a process. The Big Book describes how we were once like tornadoes roaring through people's lives. We have tried jumping into that open space before, oblivious to what was around us, like that moment of letting go when you first learn to ice skate. When we leap too soon, we may for a moment feel like we have it, that we can skate. We hang there a moment until the first twitch of a muscle causes a chain reaction of movements and reflexes that ends with us flat on our ass. The amends process should not be like that experience, where we rush in and end up flat on our ass.

We have been working slowly and methodically up to the ability to be in that open space. Can we keep in an open heart in that moment where we don't know if they are going to kiss us or kick us? This is the final stage of letting go, telling the truth about our actions to those we harmed. We do not need to have hope or fear about the outcome. Through all of our actions, the way we talk and the way we hold ourselves, we can go beyond the hope and fear of what we are trying to accomplish. Regardless of the response, we can work with it when we look at things honestly. We are endeavoring to let go of the last vestiges of self-deception. Making amends allows the stories we used to belittle ourselves with to fade away--some quickly, some slowly, but we can let go of the stories that we do not have wisdom or basic goodness within us.

When we let go we can approach the world in a different way. We all have a natural wisdom within us, our basic goodness. When the Big Book talks about "intuitively knowing how to handle situations" it is coming from this inherent wisdom that we all have inside us. This is how the Garuda flies. The Garuda flies with two wings, prajna and upaya, wisdom and skillful means. It is the combination of the two that creates the magic in situations. We have all had those moments where it seems that our behavior and our speech is almost completely different than our typical behavior and the results were wonderful. When we are done we ask ourselves, "Where did that come from?" It is those unguarded moments where we are relaxing into our own natural wisdom. We are free of our fixed mind, our habitual patterns, in an egoless fashion.

Wisdom is not just intelligence, but a combination of knowledge, experience and good judgement. Natural wisdom comes from relaxing into ourselves. I am sure we can all remember experiences that did not have the quality of good judgment, where we were not genuine. The results when we are not genuine are filled with ego and pride. We are trying to be something we are not, which results in the best-laid skillful plans crashing and burning. When we make our amends from the wrong place, from that place of ego, we are trying to force an outcome and the results are typically dreadful. It is this further relaxing, this last stage of letting go, where we discover the wisdom that we have always had within. This wisdom cannot be forced, the "desire to sharpen it will make it dull."

Step Ten

Continued to take personal inventory and when we were wrong promptly admitted it. (Big Book of AA)

Many in the rooms call the remaining steps the "maintenance" steps, claiming that to do these remaining three steps and only these three steps will keep them sober and free from addiction. The thought that these remaining three steps are all that is needed to maintain a spiritual condition which will make it impossible to drink; even if they wanted to do. They have apparently done what the Big Book of AA tells us is impossible: "No one among us has maintained anything like perfect adherence to these principles. We are not saints. The point is that we are willing to grow along spiritual lines." The previous nine steps are not one and done milestones. Character defects - check! Amends - check! It would be impossible to follow the Twelfth Step to practice these principles in all our affairs if we are only concentrating on the last three steps each day.

Yet this is a plateau of sorts. The work we are going to be doing will be of a different nature. Much of the heavy lifting and dirty work is behind us. We will, of course, discover things we left off our Fourth Step and new character defects will pop up, but now we are entering the realm of the Dragon. In many ways the realm of the Dragon is like "perfect adherence". It is a place which may be seen way off in the distance but never reached. Whether it is reachable or not is not as important as knowing that it exists, and we will have moments and glimpses of the realm of the Dragon. The Dragon has a "mind beyond mind," which gives us a clue to the possibly unachievable nature of the Dragon. Hence the Dragon is said to be inscrutable. Inscrutable can be defined as "impossible to understand or interpret."

The Dragon is a wonderful creature, not a monster, but a magical creature that can dance in the sky or on the earth. It can be any of the elements of earth, water, fire and air. Dragons are benevolent and wise. I cannot claim to be that wise, as I cannot claim to have a "mind beyond mind," but we can still use the inscrutable teachings of the Dragon to aid our recovery.

Emotional Balance

The verbiage for this step has led many to focus only on the personal inventory aspect or merely to stop and admit they were wrong. This is perfectly acceptable, as their goal is to try to keep anything from building up which would then cause them to pick up again. By doing inventories we notice where we have made mistakes which need to be repaired. We can do our inventories in the moment, daily or yearly. All types of inventories are extremely helpful, but for the moment I want to focus on the in-the-moment inventory. It is this in–the–moment noticing that leads to one of the today's buzzwords - mindfulness. A quick walk around a bookstore and you will see it everywhere. Mindfulness. Mindfulness in business, mindfulness in health, mindfulness in communicating, mindfulness and golf. It is everywhere, but it has been around since before the days of the Buddha.

So we are going to be mindful, but of what? Let's take a look at what Bill W. told us to be mindful of. When looking at the 12x12 the words that seem to repeat themselves over and over are about emotions. In the 12x12, Bill asks us, "Can we stay sober and keep in emotional balance?" Negative emotions--"anger, fear, jealousy and the like"--are what we now need to be mindful of. In a letter to the Grapevine Bill defined this a little further, terming this working with emotions as "Emotional Sobriety". How we can go through our days and have peace within ourselves regardless of the trials and turmoils of the day. As much as we wish, life is still going to happen. There will be ups and downs and now our goal is to go through these events without lapsing back into our old ways.

Basic Sobriety

Emotional Sobriety is a vital part of our ability to maintain long-term sobriety. Many of us, do not process our emotions well. In early sobriety it was overwhelming to experience all these emotions for the first time. We should lean into these uneasy emotions, little by little, like getting ourselves into a cold pool. Living here in Florida we have fewer cold pool issues, it seems, but I'm sure we can all relate to the process of getting into a cold pool--the process of little by little by little getting more of our bodies into the water, until that one moment where we have to let go and go all in. This is how we learn to deal with our emotions by slowly leaning into emotions like anger, fear, jealousy and the like.

A friend in the rooms likes to say that as we progress in our sobriety "the highs are not as high, the lows are not as low, and they don't last as long." In the beginning, I wondered about this and prayed for it to happen, hoping that each passing low would be as painful as it got. The law of karma tells that the results of past intentions and actions result in these highs and lows. Making good choices in the present, mindful decisions toward what is right, means more positive seeds being planted. Each time we go through a period of sadness we are experiencing the results of our past actions. If we do not continue the actions that created those karmas we will not continue to experience bad results. When we stop drinking or drugging or whatever it was, we still have a great momentum and fields filled with bad karma. Emotionally it seems like it is one difficult thing after another. The good thing is that with each low, the lows will get less because we are not continuing to plant the low karma seeds. As we continue on, the smaller seeds come to fruition, we experience them, and then even smaller seeds. The highs truly do not go as high and the lows do not go as low.

At any point in our sobriety there will be times where we will be completely hooked by emotions. Learning how to recognize when we are caught in these emotional distortions, the kleshas we discussed in Step Six, can help us weather the storm of our emotions. Remember, the kleshas cause our suffering because they distort our mind and perceptions. These thought distortions do not allow us to perceive reality accurately. They are the ways in which our minds convince us of things that are not really true. There are a number of these distortions and they seem to be common among people, but people in recovery seem to take these to the extreme. The following is one list of emotional distortions: all or nothing thinking, overgeneralization, filtering, disqualifying positive events, jumping to conclusions, magnification / minimization or catastrophizing, emotional reasoning, shoulding, labeling, attributing personal responsibility, blaming, fallacy of change, and always being right. Yep, sit in any Twelve Step meeting and you are bound to run into a few of these misdirected ways of thinking.

Four Reminders

Once during a weeklong silent retreat at our city center, I fell victim to a rash of distorted thinking. Today I can no longer remember what started it exactly, a look from my wife or an offhand comment. Regardless of how it began, I had started to ruminate on the slight, letting it grow and fester as I sat on the cushion next to her. Hour after hour I continued down this path of mental anguish, further enraging myself and my slighted ego. Unable to take it anymore I left the meditation hall to pace the parking lot in the hot Florida sun. Walking back and forth, I thought of numerous arguments and verbal retorts to the arguments that she would make in return. You know the scene where you try to play out all the scenarios in your head before you confront someone. There I was, completely caught up in my own melodrama, completely oblivious to the world around me, until a large leaf fluttered down before me, large and green with patches of brown. I stared at the leaf. How dare it interrupt me? The more I stared at the leaf, the more I began to see. The crystals in the asphalt next to the leaf glistened and sparkled. The edge of the concrete was white and barren. Between the two, just beyond the edge of the leaf, was a small mound of fine dirt. Little ants climbed in and out of the little mound. Little ants, so fragile and small. Ants!

If I died in that instant, if a piece of an airplane were to drop on my head, with all that anger inside me, with the resentment toward my wife still in my heart, where would I end up? Would I be lucky enough to come back as an ant? Or would I reside in some realm of hell till the anger burned up? Looking at the ants, all that anger--the ants reminded me of how fragile life is. That brought to mind the Four Reminders.

How easy to forget the little lines of the Four Reminders. The reminders are like the pithy sayings found on the walls of the rooms of recovery, little lines that can cut through our habitual patterns and wake us up, even if for just an instant. They remind us how precious this moment is. When we forget all the mindfulness of this, when we forget and believe our distorted thoughts, each of these reminders can keep us grounded.

These reminders have been passed down through the lineage, translated by Trungpa Rinpoche as:

Joyful to have such a human birth, difficult to find, free and well-favored.

But death is real, comes without warning. This body will be a corpse.

Unalterable are the laws of karma; cause and effect cannot be escaped.

Samsara is an ocean of suffering, unendurable, unbearably intense.

We have talked about suffering and karma previously, so we will only touch them briefly now. It is the first two lines that hold importance in Step Ten and are completely forgotten by most people, let alone the alcoholic addict.

Mindful of Being Human

It is said that the odds of having a human birth are as rare as a sea turtle who comes to the surface once every one hundred years, coming to the surface and putting its head through a yoke floating on an ocean that covers the entire globe. Even if you don't want to believe in reincarnation, it only takes looking around you to see how lucky we are to have been born as humans. Even with the "did you see the family I was born into" comments aside, it is fortunate to have a precious human birth.

Genetically, you are a miracle. Seven billion or so people on this earth, and there is you. You are not a snail or a ferret. You are the genetic combination of your parents, their parents, and their parents, and on and on. My siblings came from the same two sets of genetic donors and yet we are so very different in our abilities, likes, and looks. How many generations do you have to go back until we reach the proverbial genetic "Adam and Eve?" Whether we are born into the slums or with a golden spoon in our mouth, we are each something extremely rare. Our personalities and neuroses are the result of a billion karmic causes and effects, each one playing out slightly differently for each of us.

The Buddha saw the human birth as the greatest thing, because it is only in the human realm that we have the teachings of the dharma and the ability to be free of the suffering that keeps us in the loop of samsara. When we take the time to meditate, we are taking the time to appreciate who we are as human beings. When we appreciate who we are we have the potential to be totally happy. While we were in our addictions we did not appreciate this body we had or that we were human beings living another day. It is ok that we did not appreciate this human being we are; most people do not appreciate what they have in just being a human being. They think they have to be better, faster, stronger, or richer, when in fact all they have to do is be a human being. When we do so we can learn to appreciate all the wondrous aspects of the world and our life. We can appreciate the bad as well as the good. The good and the bad can help us open up to our humanity and the suffering of all beings.

The more we connect with our own sense of being a human being, the more we connect with our sense of Basic Goodness. Then as a good human being we can take responsibility for the karma and the suffering around us; we can do something outrageous and wise. We can take on the responsibility to uplift ourselves and the people around us. This is where the path of warriorship is headed. We connect with the joy of being human ourselves, and we wish we could give that gift to everyone around us. We wish we can give it to our spouses and our sons and daughters, but we cannot directly make a gift of it, because there is nothing to give. We can only help them uncover it within themselves. When we approach the world with a sense of good, all of our interactions reflect that attitude. When we feel secure in our own sense of goodness, we no longer have the need for the scheming and positioning of our old ways. This is the direction we aim, so when we stumble we do not see it as a condemnation of ourselves. We do not see ourselves as either bad or evil. No, when we begin to touch that sense of being human we know we are basically good and everything we need is right before us in the present moment.

Mindful of Death

That death is real seems to be a no-brainer, in theory anyway. Just as we forget that being a human being is a precious thing, it is imperative that we understand the reality that this body will one day be a corpse. I cannot speak explicitly about different cultures around the world, but our Western culture does not want you to think of this fact. At best our Western culture wants you to consume more and more to stave off the very thought that you will die. Look younger, healthier, thinner! No money down and 0% financing for sixty months! Most people work forty hours a week, fifty weeks a year, hoping that when they reach the "golden" age of retirement they can then travel the world, read all the books, and experience all the things that they deprived themselves of during the previous sixty-five years.

While we were living in our addiction, we may have reached a point where we hoped that the misery would end, but we drank, smoke, ate, slept with people as if death were somewhere way off in the distance, or maybe right over your shoulder. Sadly, some we know did not quite make it far enough to find recovery. For myself, there was this sense of immortality to life, particularly during the heyday of my drinking. I was good looking and carefree while drinking, spending whatever money I had, all the while ignoring what tomorrow might bring. Yet through each drunken night, I always expected to wake up the next day and do it all over again.

"Death comes at any time. We should sip life like our last drop of water." This does not mean that we hedonistically pursue pleasure without end. Neither does it mean we give up on life in this world, piously hoping to attain reward in the next. No, we begin to contemplate death so that we can remove our fear of it. We contemplate that we are going to get old, have ill health, and die. When we do this, when we wake up feeling under the weather we understand that it is merely a part of being human. The more we can remove our fear of death, the less we have to struggle to hide from it.

That we will die is extremely important for our emotional sobriety and our tenth step. This body will not last forever. Period. This is impermanence. If this body will not last forever, why do I defend it so? Why do we lament the passing of time on our bodies? In our indifference we let time slip away, ignorant of the fact that our loved ones too may die at any time. Should we let anything sit a day, a week or a month, when we can take care of it right away? This is what the tenth step reminds us to do.

Every moment has a beginning, middle and end, because of impermanence. Thousands and millions of tiny moments begin and end throughout our day. Since we cannot make anything last forever we can enjoy each of the moments through the day. We touch and let go of the emotions, knowing they will pass–unless, of course, we add the fuel of the story. Understanding that everything changes allows us to flow with the rising and falling moments through our day.

Mindful of Karma and Suffering

When we are mindful of the laws of karma, we understand that each of those impermanent moments are created from the causes and conditions that came before it. Each moment therefore provides us a choice. How do we want to go forward? What intention should we hold for the future? Knowing that each moment will bear fruit in the future, we can pause and change our course of action. Good or bad, each moment gives us everything we need in it. What we do is up to us.

The ocean of suffering, of samsara, fills the world (and all the worlds). It is endless, each grasping moment fueling the suffering in the next. We cannot avoid the suffering, but we can become less attached to the events and outcomes. What do we want to do? True, only a Buddha can completely avoid suffering, but we can change our relationship with suffering. We can use our own suffering to help us further open up to the suffering of others. We can see how we are suffering and use that suffering to understand that those around us are suffering as well. We can use suffering to further our compassion. We use our own suffering as the fuel for our journey, as we change and learn more skillful ways we can better engage the suffering of those around us.

As we go through life there is no escaping suffering. We will inevitably suffer loss of health and life. It is with the wisdom of the Dragon that we can ride the waves of our life. The choice we make will be whether we continue to grasp at situations that are not real or work with the bare nature of reality. When we understand what is occurring in our lives we can approach each moment without hope or fear. We can simply experience each moment. This is the wisdom of the dragon.

Energy of Windhorse

Who has the energy to do this daily inventory? To take our own suffering and turn that into the fuel to help others? What is the result of letting go of not only our resentments but of our attachment and grasping?

When I was drinking I had no energy. Not only was I hungover each morning, causing most of my energy to be used just to not throw up on my boss's feet, but my mind was filled with self-centered and self-serving thoughts. The world was against me and weighed a thousand pounds on my back. There was no joy in life at the end, just a string of empty days and bags of empty beer cans each night. I had no confidence in myself. My ego had been beaten and bruised. My shoulders drooped and my eyes watched the ground just beyond my feet as I walked. I slouched and slumped in my chair. I was filled with the drip of the setting sun world.

Sitting down to meditate, we position our body in an uplifted state. Our head is not drooping forward, nor are we hunched over. We are in a position of nobility and poise. Something happens right there when we sit like this. As our body settles and stills in this position, so does our mind. In this state we begin to glimpse our innate worthiness and basic goodness. When we do, we begin to discover our lungta or windhorse, a self-existing energy. Within the 10th step we have been discussing again and again the ability to work with and ride the emotions and situations of our life. This is the notion of horse. The wind principle comes from the energy of basic goodness.

When we touch that joy of being human we feel a natural energy within us. When we work with our mindfulness we strengthen our ability to ride the energy. The process of letting go of our resentments and guilt through the steps makes us joyful to be alive. This energy of windhorse is always available to us; we just need to uncover it and tune into it. When we feel this we want to share it with others, to share our joy and serenity. We've cleaned up our side of the street and we are beginning to connect with who we naturally are. This energy is always there and available to us. The more we can let go of our false self and misplaced ideas, the greater our access to this windhorse. The more we trust the basic goodness within us, the more energy we have to share with the world.

The idea that we should end each day reflecting on our actions, putting some in the good and some in the bad columns, that the Big Book mentions is also supported by the Buddhist teachings. Taking the time to reflect on our positive and negative activities and set our aspiration to improve the positive and lessen the negative allows us to set our mindset for the nighttime. Even while we are sleeping these seeds will be growing. How often our nighttime's are filled with all sorts of horrors based on our fears and anxieties of our days. Setting our intention to do better is said to help us sleep better and with more serenity. His Holiness the Seventeenth Karmapa said, "If we can go to sleep in this way, our sleep will not be useless or without purpose; it will turn into a positive state of mind, and thereby the power of what is virtuous will increase."

When We Fear and Doubt

How many times do we see that energy in the newcomer as they go through the steps? They are filled with this joyous energy and want to share it with everyone. It is truly amazing, like a new high - sobriety. Unfortunately, most times this newcomer does not know how to work with this energy. They have not settled their minds and so the energy begins to work against them. They have not learned to trust themselves, or their basic goodness, and their egos begin to find new ways to strengthen. Sure they are humble: "Let me tell you how humble I am," these newcomers shout from the rooftops. It is never too early to start the eleventh step. Bill and Bob intuited that it was now, right at this point of the tenth step, that meditation was needed and thus the eleventh step. Without a settled mind, both newcomers and people with time lose their way. They begin to have quiet, sneaky doubts. Thus they speed their lives up, filling their every waking moment to stave off the fear and doubt.

As a result of the uncertainty, in themselves and the program of the Twelve Steps, some people begin to develop a wonderful and witty logic as a way to shore up their egos and stake out their place, connecting the dots of the world and the program--anything to begin to make sense of the energy they feel, and the growing doubt. They want to show how much they understand and know, to show the old timers that they've got it and even though they do not have the twenty years of sobriety that they understand the program as those old timers do. Surely they must; they have heard each of them tell their same story over and over again each day for the seeming eternity of a few months.

Now that they have built this new fortress of logic, the fear of it being based on nothing causes fierce protection. The ego comes out in full force: "Let me tell you how bad I was... I've been to jail 3 times...6 times... 12 times..." or whatever the topic for which the one-upmanship gets played. Everyone is the worst of the worst or the best of the best of the garden variety drunks. Their humility is completely gone. Even if we are only slightly higher than the other, the necks start to reach and toes start to stretch. Newcomers and old timers each fall prey to this. The old barroom mentality of trying to one-up the other is not far from the surface.

Not surprisingly, this battle of one-upmanship takes one from the center of the group to the fringe. The "I am better than all of you" mentality takes hold and that brings a sense of loneliness. No longer a man among men, a worker among workers, they find the differences, where they are either superior or much worse. Each time they one-up; they drift farther from friendships and fellowship. They drift away from meetings. They know better than their sponsors so they drift away from sponsors and sponsees alike.

All of this generally results in a relapse and a return to old behaviors, many times with a sense of the program having let them down (ego still at play). A friend who is literally a rocket scientist likes to say, "I have seen plenty of people who were too smart for the program of recovery; I have never seen anyone who is too dumb." The Big Book starts the 5th chapter with "Rarely have we seen a person fail who has thoroughly followed our path. Those who do not recover are people who cannot or will not completely give themselves to this simple program." Having been returned to sanity, if there is a fundamental doubt in ourselves as human beings, as sober beings, then the mind will return to that fundamental doubt and people will try very hard to confuse a "simple program."

Be Teachable

Of course even writing this, that little voice inside cries out, *that is you; you just described writing your silly little book filled with logic and puzzle pieces turning a simple program into a convoluted path.* I can see myself in early sobriety falling prey to the logic and desire for my own intellect to find that one-upmanship. I remember a wonderful little woman, V., pulling me aside after a meeting and saying to me, "You want what I have, but you want it now. You want my 20 years of sobriety in your first six months" and it was true. I did want that. We drank to fit in as teenagers or at company happy hours, molding ourselves to fit in. When we get to the rooms, that behavior will be with us for a bit. Come early, stay late, they tell you. You learn the lingo and what makes people laugh. Then the doubt creeps in and the pain starts. I should be better than this, one-upping even myself.

The answer was not in going higher, but of course in becoming humble again. The answer was in realizing I did not know and setting out to find not the answer but the question--to become teachable and learn to wait for the answer. My old tendencies of wanting to be the smartest person in the room would become something to watch for. I can now chuckle at those failings, both in the rooms and in the shrine room. How many times in the first year of the Heart of Recovery did things come from a place of ego instead of a place of heart? This is part of my nightly 10th step inventory: Where did judgment become an obstacle to the wisdom of inscrutability? To even say I have achieved this mind that cannot be fathomed, that achieved space that cannot be punctured by an arrow, would be sheer arrogance. Progress not perfection, so I continue to aspire to grow in that direction.

To grow in doubtless faith in our own basic goodness can only be achieved through opening up to become a vessel for the teachings to be planted in. We grow along the path of warriorship through the sitting practice of meditation.

Step Eleven

Sought through prayer and meditation to improve our conscious contact with God as we understood Him, praying only for knowledge of His will for us and the power to carry that out. (Big Book of AA)

Trungpa Rinpoche once said, "To work for others, you first have to develop composure. If you have no basic stability, when you try to help others, they will not benefit from your help. If you are trying to prevent someone from falling out of a window, you will both go out the window together. To prevent that, you have to stay inside so you can pull them back. In order to do this, training in mindfulness and awareness is absolutely necessary."

While it is never too early to begin the practice of prayer and meditation, the founders of Alcoholics Anonymous put it here almost at the end, between the energy of refining our actions and motives of Step Ten and going forth and carrying the message in Step Twelve. In the early days of AA, the steps were accomplished in a matter of hours, not months or years. Meditation was not something that popped up as a suggestion after a long period of sobriety, but was there from the beginning. In early sobriety we are told to pray even if we do not believe and maybe meditation gets a little lip service, to merely find a few moments of quiet to begin their day. Unfortunately for many, the result is that they do not think that they can meditate when they finally try it. I recently heard a wonderful way to get children to meditate--ask them to pretend to meditate for 5 minutes. In the beginning we are told fake prayer is as good as real prayer, and the same holds true for meditation.

Yet for many, Step Eleven is what brings people into shrine rooms and meditation halls around the world. There is a false belief that the Judeo-Christians pray and the Buddhists meditate. Christians can meditate and Buddhists can pray, and some do both, pray and meditate, which is what the eleventh step is telling us to do. The common analogy in the rooms is "Prayer is talking to God, and meditation is listening to God," which gives many people the ability to do these activities in less formal ways. A walk in the woods can be both prayer and meditation for some. Others find the stillness in their favorite activity. Still others find the meeting rooms to be where they do their prayer and meditation. There are many forms of prayer and meditation. You need to find the ones that work for you. Those forms may change from time to time, but having a consistent practice is the best way to achieve results.

One workout does not get the body fit, nor does one salad suffice as a diet. The simple recommended daily prayer is to "thank your higher power for another day of life and that you remain sober today" in the morning. If you make it to the end of the day sober, then it is only proper and right to thank your higher power for helping you get through the day sober. Deepak Chopra offers the 21-day meditation challenge, with the knowledge that anything we do every day for 21 days has a good chance of becoming habit. One such "challenge" that can be helpful for newcomers to meditation is to meditate 5 minutes a day, 5 days a week for 5 weeks. Then at the end of those 5 weeks you can choose to increase the time if you so desire.

Distraction and Direction

Why do prayer and meditation work? How is it the bridge between the Tenth and the Twelfth Step? At the gut level, or kitchen sink level, newcomers are told to pray regardless of whether or not they know who they are praying to. Why? The mind can only do one thing at a time. It may seem that I can listen to music, read, walk and chew gum all at the same time, in other words, "multi-task". In fact we have become so good at multi-tasking that we cannot sit still at a stop light or wait for the doctor without TV, magazines, music and our more and more handy smartphones. The truth is our mind can only do one thing at a time, it just does it really fast. It does it so quickly that we get the impression that we are doing these things simultaneously. When we get "lost in thought" the time passes and we no longer notice the temperature around us or the growl of our stomach. At that moment, all our attention is on whatever has our attention. When we snap out of it, we suddenly notice that it is hot in the room and that we are hungry. These events were already in motion but we had momentarily forgotten to be concerned with them. In early sobriety, this is what prayer does. When we are "in prayer" we cannot also be in fear. The prayer acts as a lightning rod, grounding us in the storm of fear, bringing a few moments where we have some peace. Later, our mind then remembers the object of our fear and we are again caught in the storm of fear. So we pray again. When we do this long enough, generally we forget whatever it was that was bothering us or we move on to the next thing that is bothering us. Our day is a series of passions, aggressions and indifferences and during early sobriety the common panacea is to pray them away.

One renowned speaker in our area used to prescribe a movie as one possible panacea for our fears and problems. Go lose yourself in a movie for a few hours and see your anxiety and fear leave you for a little bit. Trungpa Rinpoche once described the experience of meditation as similar to going to the movie. When you sit down, you divide your attention into 25% to the popcorn, 50% to the movie, and 25% to everyone around you. There is a good chance you will forget to worry about your problem when your attention is already taken up by so many things in a movie. It is not that going to a movie will solve our problems, but generally worrying about our problems will not solve them either.

Buddhists Can Pray

Worrying and prayer cannot happen in the same moment. Noise, thought, sense, smells, and emotions may seem as if they are happening all at the same moment, but our mind jumps to each one bit by bit. First the sense of heat on my back, the noise of the kids playing basketball outside, the dryer running, a song playing over the computer and my own thoughts as I type. When I pause, I see the lampshade shaking behind the desk, my stomach is full from lunch, and the shadows are moving slowly across the house.

One question posed by skeptical people is whether prayer can continue to have value, now, later in the steps and later in sobriety. All the major religions use prayer as a very refined tool for spiritual communication. Whether they are communicating with God, Allah, Jesus, the Great Mystery, or the Buddha, prayer can be an active part of our continual spiritual growth. There are a great many wonderful books on prayer, and meditation for that matter, and I cannot profess to be an expert in either form. It is up to us to be watchful of whether we are using our prayer for the right reasons, or to determine our will dressed up and rationalized as "God's will."

Most of my own early thoughts about what a prayer is were either pleas to a magical being to perform absurd magic or straight-up selfish prayers. If a loved one is sick, most of the time our prayer is not really about them, but us. *I do not want to feel the pain of losing this person so please save them.* Another type of typical prayer for most of us alcoholics and addicts are the foxhole prayers to remove the trouble we found ourselves in. We bargained and pleaded; sometimes it was successful and sometimes not but chances are the promises we made on our part were quickly forgotten.

What of Buddhist prayer? In my experience there are a few types of prayer. Ideally these prayers do not ask for anything for ourselves and traditionally are more ritualized. Of course we can memorize a section from some of the great sutras or writings to use as our own prayers. Similar to the "Prayer of St. Francis", Shantideva wrote:

> *May I be a guard for those who are protectorless,*
> *A guide for those who journey on the road.*
> *For those who wish to cross the water,*
> *May I be a boat, a raft, a bridge.*

Basic Sobriety

May I be an isle for those who yearn for land,
A lamp for those who long for light;
For all who need a resting place, a bed;
For those who need a servant, may I be their slave.

We can remember these inspirational words or ones similar. Other forms of prayer can be more traditional, like morning and evening chants. At the time of the Buddha there were no recordings or even books. The teachings were continued and passed on orally. Chanting was a method for memorization. Much like how we can continue to recall a popular song even when it has been years since we last heard it, chanting engages a different portion of our brain and memory. Ask me the address I lived at for 5 years before I got sober and I will look back at you with a blank stare, but we can all remember songs from decades ago. The chants hold teachings. As we chant, the words enter our mind, maybe not at a conscious level at first, but they penetrate us. Each time we chant, they get embedded a little deeper, so that in times of need and troubles the teachings are there for us.

Chanting resonates within you. The tone, the speed, the vibrations all get inside you. The vibrations work with the words to touch you on a deeper level. People with a lot more letters after their names can tell you why that is, but just in the simple act of humming a low tone for the length of a breath you can feel that something is happening. That is what we are doing: we are feeling the words beyond the meanings. We are taking them from the realm of the intellect and placing them within our body and heart. The teachings are held within the chants and we need to take the teachings from our mind and be able to feel them, to embody them. The "Aspiration of Shambhala" chant that is said at the close of each day is a reminder of all the pithy instructions and teachings of Shambhala. Everything is within this single chant: the reminders of unconditional goodness, the dignities, the preciousness of life and the direction we wish to strive in our own personal lives and the life of the lineage.

The Power of Prayer

So who are we praying to? And why? Many times, a traditional form of meditation or practice utilizes visualizations. We hold an image in our mind, or in our body, or we imagine in our mind something in our body, and this helps to strengthen our focus and intention. When we take the refuge vow we hold an image of the Buddha in our mind throughout the practice. Doing so reminds us of our own Buddha nature that we intrinsically have. We are not asking for a mystical Buddha on high to magically move heaven and earth for us, but for our own understanding of our own true nature. When we pray we are connecting with the pieces of ourselves that we, at that moment, are having difficulty finding within ourselves. Everything we need is found within us and within each moment. Everything right where we are has everything we need to awaken our enlightened essence, an essence that lies within us already. Praying for patience or the ability to forgive someone is not asking someone outside ourselves to grant these qualities to us, but is so that we can rediscover those qualities already within us.

If there is no duality and no non-duality and we are all interconnected, our prayers have a power greater than we can understand. Outer and inner go together; there is no separation between the two. It is only our own concepts that divide the two. Even though we may feel we are praying to something outside of ourselves we are in actuality praying to our own wisdom consciousness. This consciousness is always available; however, at times we feel that we are unable to connect to it. In times of trouble and anxiety we can call on the strength of people who have already passed away or who are far away. We can recall their images and words and truly feel their strength. We may not be able to see the power of a prayer, but we know from karma that an intention is never forgotten. An intention always bears fruit. When we pray, we are putting forth good energy into the universe. Praying for a loved one to be healed, or a lost child to be found, or that a region recover from a natural disaster, will all bear fruit in some way.

Within our daily sobriety, in the rooms there are two typical prayer responses to problems. The first is for you to pray for the other person when you have a problem with someone. The second is that regardless of the problem the answer is to "pray on it". The first is a valuable tool to help us open our own heart, the second can be a tool used to avoid and not deal with our problems.

The typical advice for when we are having issues with another person is to pray for the other person for 14-21 days. Earlier, I mentioned that 21 days has the chance to become a habit (although with alcoholics and addicts it could be much longer than that, depending on the subject of the action). Praying for someone for 21 days has the chance to turn our anger into compassion, our fear into understanding, or our stubbornness into acceptance. In Step Eight we discussed how what changes is us, not them. However, the change in us reflects off the surfaces of the world, including that person. Our change has the possibility of creating a change in the other person. Our kindness may one day be reflected by them. We change the thing we can, which is us, and as a result our view of others and how we interact with them changes.

When we are faced with a problem prayer can be a very powerful tool, but we need to combine it with action. In some cases prayer has been known to do some very amazing things. There are stories about people praying away cancer and other horrible illnesses. I cannot say that if you pray that these things will happen, and I cannot say that prayer will have no power. Just the action of praying for someone could change everything--within us, at least. In previous steps we have discussed numerous forms, practices and methods of "prayer" that work to open our heart. Prayer is a tool to help us work with our problems and emotions, not to avoid them. The Buddha's instructions for all of his teachings hold true here as well: "Try it and see what happens." Sending positive energy into the universe surely cannot hurt.

Prayer is not so much about us. As much as our old prayers were to save our own asses, we need to change our outlook. Remember, the Big Book states, "We ask especially for freedom from self-will, and are careful to make no requests for ourselves only. We may ask for ourselves, however, if others will be helped. We are careful never to pray for our own selfish ends." So in fact the type of prayer recommended by the Big Book is not about ourselves at all. Thus prayer is the groundwork for Step Twelve.

Thomas Merton said in *New Seeds of Contemplation*:

> *He who attempts to act and do things for others and for the world without deepening his own self-understanding, freedom, integrity and capacity to love, will not have anything to give others. He will communicate to them only the contagion of his own obsessions, his aggressiveness, his ego-centered ambitions, his delusions about ends and means, and his doctrinaire prejudices and ideas.*

A Long Lineage

To know the proper actions to take, we must sit in meditation. But what is meditation exactly? There is the act of what we think we are doing, and what we are doing, and what we should really be doing. Yet for all it is and all it really is not, it is a powerful tool whose goal is an "entire psychic change." For without this change there may be little hope for recovery.

Chogyam Trunpga said, "In regard to meditation, if one begins to enjoy it, then there must be some kind of entertainment going on, which is quite fishy."

Every time my daughter or son says to me, "I'm bored!" my internal response, and sometimes external response, is "How wonderful, now try to sit with it." On one level this is what we are trying to find, boredom. Our mind does not like to be bored. It goes to elaborate lengths to keep this from happening. Corporations have keyed in on this. Disney World no longer wants you to be bored while you are standing in line, so you can pay extra money to not have to stand around. Notice your own mind when you are at a stop light, waiting. Meditation is asking us to buck that trend of our mind. A watched pot never boils, but here, in essence we are going to watch the pot never boil. We are going to court boredom. Why, you ask? Well, boredom is only temporary for one and we go through a stage of hot boredom, which is the waiting at the light kind, of waiting for the bell to ring, to a stage of cool boredom, in which we are all right with the boredom. More importantly, we know that we are not doing anything.

Sitting is sitting. Sit fully and simply. You are not going anywhere. You are not out to out-meditate the guy sitting next to you. You are not there to prove anything or achieve anything. *Today I am really going to hit it out of the park; I am going to reach enlightenment. Yesterday's meditation was bad, but today's is going to be really good.* We need to leave all of that stuff at the door, or they will be the thoughts that become obstacles. Expectations of results will ultimately hamper our journey. What we need to do is learn that we do not have to do anything, that being as we are and where we are is good. Perfectly good.

It is very important to know what type of practitioners we are following. In the beginning of the book there is a background of who Chogyam Trungpa Rinpoche was. He was the holder of two lineages of Tibetan Buddhism, the Kagyu and Nyingma. The Kagyu and Nyingma lineages are two of the six main lineages in Tibetan Buddhism. Each of the lineages has its own flavor of teachings, styles and interpretation. They are all derived from the same source but with different emphasis on different aspects. One of the main characteristics of the Kagyu lineage is that it emphasizes the direct transmission of the oral teachings from teacher to student, teaching the spontaneous insight of enlightened realization.

The Kagyu lineage is a practice lineage. The practice of sitting meditation is emphasized from the beginning and remains a core practice along the path to liberation. Without the practice of sitting meditation, all of the teachings will remain in our heads, not in our hearts or as the Tibetans refer to it the "heart/mind," which is in the center of our chest.

The Nyingma lineage is an ancient lineage, which is a little more scholarly than the practical, practicing Kagyupas. The Nyingma lineage too practices sutra and tantra teachings, with an additional focus on the Dzogchen teachings and the compassion of Padmasambhava. An interesting thing about Padmasambhava is that he and his consort Yeshe Tsogyal placed teachings to be discovered in the future. Over the decades, hundreds of such hidden teachings, called terma, have been found by tantric masters. The Shambhala teachings are terma teachings discovered by Chogyam Trungpa. Terma are to be found by the proper teacher when the teachings are most needed. Our current lineage holder, Sakyong Mipham Rinpoche, studied under his father Shambhala, Kagyu and many great Nyingma teachers and is considered the reincarnation of Mipham the Great, a Nyingma scholar and master.

Shambhala combines these two lineages along with the Shambhala terma, resulting in a series of meditation practices which help the student progress through the hinayana, mahayana, and vajrayana teachings. It is through the sitting practice of meditation that we can experience our basic goodness. When we practice meditation we discover our innate worthiness, which is complete and wholesome. By practicing to be fully with our breath, we learn to fully appreciate our present moment experience, or nowness. We are on the cushion as we are, just as we are. Our good and bad can sit together, neither applauding or rejecting any aspect of ourselves. Applying gentleness and inquisitiveness, we can explore what it truly feels like for each of us in our experience. We are not trying to get anything from outside ourselves but to rediscover our true nature, which is awake and good.

Meditation is Not About the Cushion

Learning to sit peacefully with our own mind, we begin to understand its nature, how it reacts to our thoughts, creating emotions from the stories we tell ourselves. We do not need to be thrown from our seat by our emotions, but a peaceful mind allows for the emotions to exist without manipulation or rejection. We simply feel how we feel, being who we are in that moment. Meditation is an act of bravery and nobility. When we sit, we sit with purpose of being and a sense of energy. We are warriors in the world and the battle begins within each of us. Learning to abide with our emotions, we no longer have to battle or fight with ourselves; as a result, we become all victorious.

When we rise from our cushion we take our meditative mind with us out into the world. Whether we are walking, running, doing the laundry or eating a meal, we can take our mind of awareness and kindness with us. Meditation is not about the cushion. We need life to push our buttons, so that we can work with the energies that arise within us. There is no need to convince a fish that water is wet. It is about life. If there was no turbulent mind, there would be no possibility of a peaceful mind. If we only had a peaceful mind, there would be no need for meditation. Meditation does not need to end because we are living our life. When our mind is stable enough we can drop the technique of being with the sense of breathing and just be in the world. Whatever activity we are doing, we can do it fully and wholly. Trungpa taught that life is full of daily rituals: the getting out of bed ritual, the brushing our teeth ritual, the walking into the office ritual, etc., and all of the rituals can be treated with a sense of dignity and awareness. Synchronizing body and mind allows us to be present and aware with all our rituals throughout the day, appreciating the uniqueness of each moment.

It is only off the cushion that the work of meditation bears fruition. Wisdom gained on the cushion means little if we cannot take it out into the world. Being "enlightened" means little if we are an asshole out in the world. Further, if we did not learn to work with the doubt and uncertainty that is bound to crop up in our self-criticizing mind, we would not be able to help anyone. The direction we need to go is plain to see: we need to help others. We need to be off the me plan. If we rush right into helping others, we may stay sober another day, but our helping may be doing more harm than good. Sure, the Big Book makes it seem easy, that given a few hours we can surely convince the newcomer that we know all about the "alcohol game" and be able to change the course of their lives. Is it that easy?

In a world of constant entertainment many expect there to be more to the practice of meditation. Even the simple instruction given to newcomers has been greatly thought out and hidden within its simplicity are profound teachings. There are many different techniques of meditation. One style of meditation may be helpful when our mind is racy, while another will be more useful during more settled times. These techniques fall within the path of "hearing, contemplating and meditating." A process that relates to the eleventh step and the ideas held within the step of "knowledge of His will for us and the power to carry that out".

Hearing, Contemplating, Meditating

We need to go through the process of hearing, contemplating and meditating to bring the whole thing out of our logic-run, self-centered brain and into our caring, gentle heart. Where we begin is by hearing the instructions for meditation. The first time we hear the instructions we think, *I got this* and rush off and go sit, hoping for enlightenment. Mostly we listen to things. We listen to people talk, the radio and the television. We say we are giving our attention to the sounds, but we are not perceiving the sounds. This reminds me of reading the instructions to a new game. You read over the instructions and they all seem to make sense. There is a vague understanding of what happens when, but there is no understanding why things happen until you sit down and start playing the game.

Basic Sobriety

Somewhere along the way we start to notice the subtle nuances that go into playing the game. Now we are beginning to understand what we read, and reread, and read again. The same process happened when we listened to people for years tell us that we had a problem; it was only when we started to actually hear them that it began to penetrate our minds and egos.

The most common form of meditation taught at Shambhala centers is shamatha meditation. This is a method to help us reduce our thoughts and gain stability. This is a mindfulness practice which uses a single point of focus, our body breathing. The mindfulness is not a process or external element; it already exists within us. We begin with the body breathing, because it is there, constantly there. It gives our restless minds, which are typically jumping all about, something to keep coming back to, something or somewhere to take a rest. We are not trying to control anything, merely trying to uncover what already exists. We begin with our body and the sense of breathing because most of the time we completely forget we even have a body unless we bump into something or something aches. Within shamatha meditation we uncover a sense of mindfulness and awareness. Mindfulness is the realization that we are no longer following the sense of our body breathing. Once we realize we are gone, it is our awareness that reminds us to come back. Very simple? Now we do it a few million times, or so it seems. No matter which Buddhist lineage you practice, many begin with shamatha meditation. Shamatha meditation was the form that the Buddha was working with before and after his moment of enlightenment.

The directions for meditation are relatively simple, or so we first feel. Yet when we first sit down we discover that a) we have completely forgotten the instructions--"What were the instructions again?" and b) we have a lot of thoughts. Once we have settled our minds a bit, we can begin to actually use thoughts to aid our journey. Sadly, what we should have for lunch will not get us very far on our spiritual journey of awakening. If we are trying to go on a spiritual journey it helps to contemplate spiritual teachings. We can contemplate bigger issues like the four reminders, the four immeasurables, a line or two from a spiritual book, or a daily reflection. By doing this we engage our meditative practice. It is through contemplation that we begin to make changes within ourselves. When we are contemplating we use our thoughts as the focus of our meditation. We let the words soften our mind. When we first began sitting our mind was very rigid and hard. Shamatha meditation softens our minds, then contemplating is like planting the seeds. When we can let go of our own preconceived concepts of what we think something means, we can open up to the words and actually begin to hear them. It is then that our innate wisdom comes forth and we begin to understand in a different manner. We allow whatever arises to arise without our trying to manipulate it. After our contemplation period we come back to meditating on our breath to stabilize our mind, so that we do not start laying conception and ego onto our thoughts. Remember there are no good thoughts or bad thoughts. It is this process that will begin to change us.

In one of the rooms I first got sober in is a handwritten sign: "If I don't change, my sobriety date will." Yet, for all the fancy calligraphy slogans that lined the walls--"Live and Let Live; Think, Think, Think; Let Go and Let God," etc.--it was this simple handwritten one that always struck me like a lightning bolt. Each time I found myself in that room, in those first days and weeks of my sobriety, I would reread that line dozens of times. I was terrified of drinking again and there was the answer - change. My sponsor reiterated the sentiment, over and over again, that if I wanted to remain sober I needed to do a complete 180-degree change from who I once was.

Inscrutability

The inscrutable wisdom of the dragon is that there is a natural logic to this "difficult to understand" wisdom. This logic relates to not only to our training as warriors in the world, but to our place in the steps of transition from self to other. The logic of inscrutability is divided into four stages. The first stage is awareness. We should develop awareness of ourselves and the world around us, wholly and fully. This awareness is the understanding of how we relate to ourselves and the world. This is our tenth step practice, seeing how we related to ourselves and others throughout our day, and since nothing is off the path, even how we related to the kitchen sink full of dishes is important.

The next stage of inscrutability is belief. We are not trying to believe in grandiose theories of how everything works but simple and straightforward theories that work in our daily lives and interactions. We drop the stories, we learn to see things as they are, and as we talked earlier about destroying our sense of victimhood, we begin to deal with things simply and directly. When we are dealing with things simply and directly we develop a sense of fearlessness, which is the third stage. We do not have to run away and hide when we have fear any more, we are learning to work with all of our emotions, so we can have fear and fearlessness at the same moment. Both are ok. We do not have to reject one in favor of the other. As a result we begin to "be on the spot." Being on the spot is a powerful place in that we have our awareness of our fear and we work with our own fear as part of the situation. We are there, open, without any big theories of how things should unfold, which allows anything to happen.

The final stage is action--the "intuitively know how to handle situations" type of action without forethought or concept. In this final stage, our actions will be inscrutable due to our wisdom and directness. We will not be perfect in this we must remember progress, not perfection. All of these stages are guideposts of progress toward a seemingly unattainable perfection. Yet we will have moments or periods of all of this coming together. Moments here and there where I look back and wonder, "Where did that come from? When out of nowhere I react in a completely unexpected fashion to a situation and everything just flows and works for the benefit of someone else.

Sacred World

Through the process of the steps, the path and meditation we have been looking at different ways that we can open up to the idea of emptiness within ourselves. This emptiness is not devoid of anything, but rather it is empty of the ideas that I have created for it. I am not what I think I am, the construct of all these pieces and parts that my mind likes to gather together and call me. The more we can understand in our hearts the truth of this, the more we can begin to see that the world is not such a horrible place. Our loving-kindness that we develop within us begins to grow into compassion for others. This is the growth stage of the process. First we take a bit of our focus off ourselves and we become curious about the world around us. What we discover is not what we thought the world was but how the world is around us. The world around us is sacred and full of magic and meaning. We have been so wrapped up in our own problems and dramas that we failed to notice the world around us.

As we grow in mindfulness of what is occurring within us we begin to naturally nurture and care for the world around us. This care begins in our homes. How we keep our bedroom or our even closets begins to influence the world around us. Caring for our belongings and the spaces around us can grow into an appreciation of the sacred world around us. It is only through touching on the "emptiness" of our own being that we can begin to see the sacredness around us. The world around is rich and full, yet when completely engrossed with our own lives we barely notice. We hardly get out into the world to explore it.

Simple acts of caring for the world around us are the seeds that will bear fruit in the future. This attention and care for our world is how we discover its self-existing beauty. We do not wear our shoes on our heads. Understanding this simple logic helps us to see the beauty of the world around us. When things are being used in their right and proper manner, they flow naturally. We do not need to fill our world with lavish material possessions, but to care for and understand the value of the items we do have in our life manifests in a sense of elegance. Making the bed, washing the dishes, putting our clothes away allows us to appreciate the world around us.

This is the brink of the Twelfth Step. The Eleventh Step takes us to that open space of awareness and tenderness. Yet we can't just float off into that space. All of this calls for returning to the ground. "The monarch with a broken heart" cannot live in his self-contained Eden when there are so many people hurting in the world. We cannot ignore the world, now that we are free from much of our own suffering. We must take our kit of spiritual tools and help others. We must carry the message.

Step Twelve

Having had a spiritual awakening as the result of these steps, we tried to carry this message to other alcoholics, and to practice these principles in all our affairs. (Big Book of AA)

What is the purpose of the Twelve Steps? For some, it is merely to get sober. Is that not what is read at the start of (most) every meeting?

"Sobriety, freedom from alcohol through the teaching and practicing of the Twelve Steps is the sole purpose of an AA group."

So why the Twelfth Step? When Ebby brought the message to Bill that fateful night the twelfth step was laid out as Bill W. writes:
"My friend had emphasized the absolute necessity of demonstrating these principles in all my affairs. Particularly was it imperative to work with others as he had worked with me." This was to be the foundation of the program.
Many say that the purpose of the program is to have a spiritual awakening, for without a spiritual awakening one would not have the faith to remain free of addiction. Addiction is indeed a subtle and tricky foe. I am not discounting the spiritual awakening aspect. I am merely posing that there is something else at play here. A spiritual awakening is wonderful, yet that would fall short, for as Bill continues:
"For if an alcoholic failed to perfect and enlarge his spiritual life through work and self-sacrifice for others he could not survive the certain trails and low spots ahead."
So the singular spiritual awakening is not enough; we must continue forward. Or as the Sakyong says, "We need to get off the me plan" if we are going to remain sober.

Basic Sobriety

Helping Others

Practical experience shows that nothing will so much insure immunity from drinking as intensive work with other alcoholics. It works when other activities fail. (p.89, Big Book, Chapter 7- Working with Others.)

"Nothing will" was a phrase that hit me square between the eyes in my early sobriety. Nothing. One day even my spirituality will fail. Let me repeat: "my" spirituality will fail, that's small "me" will fail. I will get complacent, egocentric or lazy and I will lose my connection to "my higher power." It will not be that any of it--higher power, faith, spirituality or the Twelve Steps will fail me--it will be me who will fail it and in turn I will fail my sobriety. The Big Book tells me that when I am spiritually fit I can go and do anything--except drink, of course. The problem is, I am probably a really bad judge of my own sense of spiritual fitness.

Of course carrying the message is not so easy as running off to the nearest drunk tank and preaching the benefits of sobriety to relieve our own unease. No, we need to have something to give away first, something that shows that the whole system works. We need to work on ourselves, through the first ten steps, develop stability and wisdom in Step Eleven, then we can begin to help others in a real and meaningful way. However, if you did run off to a detox or a rehab to help out or to share your story early in sobriety, that is wonderful. To someone sitting in detox or new to rehab someone with thirty years of sobriety may not seem real or believable, more like a unicorn than a real person. The hardest thing, for me, before I got sober was to believe that it was possible to live a day without drinking (and be happy about it). If you have a day, a week, or a month, to the newcomer you have something they want. They want the hope that they too can just put a day or a mere week between them and a drink. A week ago you may have been sitting in that same detox, just like them and look at you now.

The direction of carrying the message works in a variety of ways. Yes, there is the sponsor to sponsee or old timer to newcomer framework, but there is also the newcomer to old timer direction. What the newcomer is sharing is their own insanity, which does a great deal to help people with time. The reminder of how things once were is a very powerful message to receive from the newcomer.

We all can relate to the excitement of the newcomer who is so thrilled with their own sobriety that they want to give that joy to everyone, alcoholics and non-alcoholics alike. Even our own first attempts to get a sponsee are so filled with the desire to help and be of service that we really have no clue what we are doing. The 12x12 gives a gentle seat to rest on while we are gaining our credibility as human beings, for the 12x12 states that going to meetings and participating is valid Twelfth Step work. However, given the emphasis placed on this work, helping others was intended to be a much more active part of our recovery.

Our very lives, as ex-problem drinkers, depend upon our constant thought of others and how we may help meet their needs.

"Our very lives" is another dramatic statement, but considering the length of time that some of us downplayed our addiction it is only through statements like this that we begin to see the severity of the problem. Left to our own devices we are probably not going to want to put ourselves out there the way the Big Book describes. It is not a surprise that we need to be thinking of others, as Bill sprinkles this sentiment throughout the Big Book. Long before we reach Step Twelve helping others is in the Third Step prayer and then when we are done cleaning up the wreckage of the past, Bill hits that sentiment again in Steps Ten and Eleven.

"...the truth that faith alone is insufficient. To be vital, faith must be accompanied by self-sacrifice and unselfish, constructive action."

It is the going from the selfish and self-centered to self-sacrificing and unselfish that is the mark of our spiritual awakening. We are not just trying to achieve sobriety; we all had snippets of that before - we called it being dry. Being dry sucked. Sobriety alone will not be enough; we are after a happy sobriety. Happy, joyous and free! Right? From the Tenth Step the 12x12 tells us, "It is a spiritual axiom that every time we are disturbed, no matter what the cause, there is something wrong with us," but that does not equal happiness. What is not so self-evident is that if I want to be happy, truly happy, I can only achieve that by helping others. There is nothing I can accumulate, get, earn, possess, or desire that will ultimately make me happy. All of those things will ultimately bring pain, jealousy, attachment and loss. Another way to look at would be that the first ten steps get the soil ready, eleven plants the seeds and the fruition is in Step Twelve.

After the Buddha arose from his enlightenment, at first he did not share his findings. Others wouldn't understand, he thought. They would not be able to see what he saw. For a few days it is said that he wandered around, all by himself, enjoying whatever one experiences when one is completely awake and enlightened. Then he saw that he could not keep what he found to himself, that even if they did not understand he needed to try. Ending our own suffering is one thing, actually a very selfish thing, but to have compassion for others and want to end their suffering--now that is something special. The desire to end the suffering of others may be the supreme thought, the greatest thought one might have. So for the next 40 years or so the Buddha taught. He taught all sorts of people, kings and beggars, arhats and murderers, trying to help them to end their own suffering.

A friend reminds me, "The most selfish thing we can do today is drink. It is basically saying to all those around me that their suffering is not important. That their happiness is not important, but my suffering is important and to end my suffering I am going to drink." When we drank we spread misery and sadness. Just being sober means that those around us will not have that particular sadness and misery. If we can help another family feel that way, if we can help another see the "sunshine of the spirit" or the beauty of the world, should we deny them? Should we only try to ease the pain and suffering for alcoholics and addicts?

No One is Exempt

Everyone is suffering. Everything is not just love and light. Your wife and child are suffering, not just because they live with an alcoholic or addict, but because they are human. Sure, we've made our amends to them, but they still suffer. Would you want your child (wife, partner, mother, father, dog or insert any name you want here) to be free of suffering if you could? What about the family next door? Should only your household not suffer? The family next door also has loved ones and is loved by others who may or may not be alcoholics. Somewhat silly, is it not? This idea that I would be ok with some people suffering while I am concerned with helping other people not suffer. They might not be alcoholic or addicts, but everyone has to deal with the first noble truth. There will be suffering.

Can we do anything to help them? Ourselves? This is what we have been doing. The hinayana teachings work on the premise that to help others we must begin by working on ourselves. By working on ourselves the world around us is improved. Pretty easy to see logic. Sobriety has made the world a much brighter place for so many people. Police and emergency room nurses are all grateful for those of us needing sobriety finding it. Our homes are happier; our spouses and children are happier. Each of the steps we have worked has been helping us along this route, by removing guilt and shame, defects of character and shortcomings. We have worked hard to make things better. We smile at the world and the world will for the most part smile back a bit (thank you, karma).

This is not enough. Our own little bubble one day would most likely burst, a bad case of the fuck-its and we're off to the nearest liquor store. No, even in the preface to the 2nd edition it states, "It also indicated that strenuous work, one alcoholic to another, was vital to permanent recovery." We always wanted the easier, softer way, so the idea of strenuous work really puts a cramp in our style. If it was not vital to our permanent recovery, we would probably not do it at all.

Awakened Heart

The mahayana teachings say that we can rouse the right motivation to involve ourselves in the world with a sense of benevolence, fearlessness and kindness on a relative level. On the ultimate level we discover a larger sense of emptiness, which allows us to see that there is no separation between anyone or anything. That guy on the corner, passed out, is me. I am also that guy. When we discover a sense of emptiness, we can begin to let go a little of this great "I" that I so want to protect. When we discover this openness within ourselves we are less afraid that the world will take what we need. Understanding that we already have everything we need allows us to let go of our lord of the manor mentality of "MINE!"

We have been working through the steps to reach the point of "having had a spiritual experience" or in Buddhist terms we are trying to reach a point of "Awakened Heart" or bodhichitta. This is the goal. It is greater than enlightenment. Achieving enlightenment for ourselves only would be the ultimate "MINE!" and "Fuck you all!" That would be the ultimate selfishness. No, to work for the sake of others--that is true compassion. To care enough for those around us to say, "No matter what happens, I am not going to cross the finish line of enlightenment until all sentient beings do so"--now that is a great wish. To do so we need to touch on a great sense of compassion and tenderness. We must open our hearts to put the needs of others before our own.

Throughout the steps we have been either formally or informally working toward this goal--to get off the me plan and think about others. Lojong, tonglen, maitri, the skandhas have all been means by which we have tried to take "me" less seriously. Knowing that there is not a solid, unchanging, permanent "self," the bodhisattva can give up a little ground each day. The tool that the bodhisattva uses to help further awaken his or her heart is the six paramitas, which we discussed in Step Eight. Whereas before we looked how the paramitas aided our recovery, now we are using them as vehicles to be of service to our fellow man. Each day we can hold the aspiration to help others in our heart. We may not be perfect, but if we keep reminding ourselves, if we keep aspiring to help others, maybe some days we will.

To seal the deal we can make a vow to help others, if we so desire. This is the culmination and the beginning of the Mahayana Buddhist path. We arouse the wish to help others and awaken our minds and hearts, both the beginning and fruition of the step is achieving an ultimate state of helping ourselves and others to reach enlightenment. I know in our American culture we do not take vows and oaths completely seriously. "I swear to tell the whole truth and nothing but the truth…" can be a laughable statement at times. Yet if we are serious about our commitment to want to help others, we have already done a great deal of work to prepare for this.

What Next

Throughout the steps we have been discussing how meditation and warrior practices can be vital parts of our recovery and development. As we learn to connect with our own selves, our bodies and feelings, learning to just rest and accept however we are in the moment, we are beginning to touch the preciousness of life. The uniqueness of each individual moment, each breath, each day, is something to be celebrated. Ok, we do not get the ticker tape parade for another day being sober, but we do need to understand what a special thing we are experiencing. While in our addiction we trudged through our days, one after another, oblivious to the special qualities and magic of each moment. Today we can experience how each breath is different from the one before it. We may feel that not much changes from day to day, hour to hour, but we know that nothing is ever the same.

Basic Sobriety

The reality that nothing is ever the same is included in the idea of ceremony. Ceremony is not just something formal or repetitive. While it may seem that we repeat the same series of actions over and over again, in fact, it is like the breath; it is not repetitive at all. This is what makes each ceremony so meaningful and significant. If we hold in our heart the uniqueness of every moment, then simple acts of making coffee, washing the dishes, or walking to the bathroom each become the small ceremonies that make up our lives. When we can see the goodness in our own being, we can see each of these ceremonies as an act of that goodness.

Celebration, on the other hand, typically involves ceremony on a larger scale. Here the scale is not number of people, but in terms of range. We celebrate the change of seasons, and years, the rise and fall of each day, the natural order of things. Celebration does not solely mean toasts and party hats, but honoring the importance of events in our lives. Celebration is the feeling of fundamental goodness and healthiness of a moment. Humanity has lost a connection to this kind of celebration. We "celebrate" the New Year by getting all dressed up and getting drunk, forcing ourselves to be "happy" because that is what we are told we are supposed to be. No, celebration is the joy of the uniqueness of the moment.

Taken together, these expressions of goodness through meditation, warrior practices, ceremony and celebration are the tools that the warrior brings into the world, into society. The Big Book says, "Deep down in every man, woman, and child, is the fundamental idea of God", so too is the idea that deep down inside, every man, woman and child wants to live in a good human society. Deep down inside each of us is basic goodness, which means that each of us is fundamentally enlightened already. When we connect with our own sense of basic goodness we begin to connect with it in other people. It is already there in each of us; it is already there in everyone out there. Society is the living ceremony of humanity. If each human is already enlightened then humanity is already enlightened. If society is made up of people, already enlightened people, then society itself is already enlightened. It just does not know it yet.

This is the warrior's vow. The warrior's vow is to help society awaken to its own state of goodness. The warrior vows to create an Enlightened Society, a good human society, on this earth, in this lifetime.

Enlightened Society

This idea of an Enlightened society is not the desire to create a utopian society. The idea is rooted in the enlightened societies of Shambhala and the kingdom of Gesar of Ling. The beginning of the kingdom of Shambhala occurred when its king had gone to the Buddha to ask for teachings, but could not leave his people for his own salvation, so instead asked the Buddha for teachings on how to rule his people. Gesar of Ling was a legendary Tibetan ruler said to have lived in the 12th century. Gesar defeated many armies so that his people could live in peace and happiness.

What happened in both these societies was not that everyone achieved enlightenment, but that there was a fundamental shift in how the members of these societies interacted with one another. It was not that there were no bad events or bad actions committed within these societies, but that the society worked from a ground of goodness. When the pieces of the society understood that their inner nature was healthy and pure, how they interacted with one another came from that place of goodness as well. Instead of looking at everyone around them as evil and out to get them, they saw that they and everyone around them were inherently and basically good.

How would we live if we came not from a place of "original sin" but a place of good? As alcoholics and addicts, it is extremely difficult for us to look at the wreckage of our past and present and reconcile this. *If I am good, how could I have done all the things that I did that hurt so many people? If I am good, how could so many bad things befall me?* The steps certainly have helped us to feel better about our past and our present. Meditation has allowed us the glimpse that we possess this basic goodness. Through our sobriety and meditation we have learned to allow our emotions and experiences of the world to exist. When we see that our experience of the world is an experience of the world without story or overlay, then we begin to trust that our sense of self is authentic and worthy of respect.

Finding time to connect to ourselves and to others through feeling is foundational for creating enlightened society. Sharing joy, sorrow, tenderness and excitement builds relationship with others; learning to truly listen is the key. Doing so with kindness and gentleness ensures that we can honor our connection with others in a way that builds genuine community.

It may not be perfect, but this is why we feel so different after a meeting. A recovery room, on a good day, is a good, genuine human community. You often hear people joke about how they wish everyone had a recovery community to turn to, to listen and to share with, the way that we do. It is not an ideal situation, as some people hurt and are going through tough times without any support or feel that they cannot reach out to others until they are ok themselves. Enlightened Society is not so much about creating a perfect world in which there is never anything bad happening. Enlightened Society is a real working society, maybe very much like the one we are living in today. The difference might just be in how we view ourselves and one another.

Can we relieve the suffering of the world? What is your own personal idea of what an enlightened society might look like? How might we get there? These are all questions we must ask ourselves individually and collectively. The world has tried to discover peace through war, serenity through chaos and purity through pollution. I believe it was the Dalai Lama who said something to the effect of "If we could achieve peace through war, like we have the past thousands of years, by all means we should devote all our resources to war. However, that has not worked nor will it work. We must try a different way to find peace." That is the thing: this view of our world today does not work. It is not all bad; there are good bits, but as a collective whole at the moment it does not work. The direction we are headed is what is considered the darkest of dark times. It is hard to see how our planet can continue the way it is going and survive.

So what can we do? We did not get sober to be miserable. No, we discovered that a life free from numbness and addiction can be a wonderful thing. We need to share it. It radiates from us. A friend who likes to go on cruises always goes to the Friends of Bill meetings. He take his Big Book and finds the room, usually in some out of the way corner of the ship. He knows how important it is to hold that seat, to be the best example of the Big Book he can be, for the person who comes may not know anything about AA, the Big Book or the fellowship, therefore it is through who he is, "attraction not promotion," that can show them how it all can work. This is the mentality of the Enlightened Warrior. We must radiate the kindness and compassion we want the world to be, a world in which we are safe to simply be.

Enlightened society begins with each of us. We cannot just go rushing out into the world and expect to make things change in a positive manner. No, we discussed that in Step Eleven: we must stabilize our own mind and connect with our own basic goodness before we can begin to help others. Much like the Big Book addresses the family, in the chapter "To the Family" we begin with the home. Can we uplift our own home? Can our homes become examples of the Shambhala teachings and principles? We begin with ourselves and then the next step is our households. For many in recovery this, the family, is the most difficult aspect of sobriety. It is here that our buttons will be pushed, because they installed the buttons, and here that we will be tested if we are practicing these principles in all our affairs. Regardless of what your home and family life consists of, we can approach it with a sense of dignity and grace.

"Wife or no wife, job or no job," we can still live a dignified, meaningful life. If you have a family living with you under one roof, great! If you are an example of the non-nuclear family, great! Single? Great! We start where we are with what we have. We do not need a 2,000 square foot home with a two-car garage and a dog before we develop our enlightened society. If you have a jeans and t-shirt lifestyle we can still wear them with dignity and grace. We can be awake to all the little ceremonies that we enact in our homes. We do not need to have the most expensive objects, but we can choose our furnishings and decor by paying attention to style and quality. A simple elegant bowl displayed in the center of a table has a natural power and dignity. That same bowl next to 15 other knick-knacks and other *objects d'art* may be individually a wonderful piece but it gets lost among all the clutter.

Our home becomes the center of our mandala. We are each the center of our mandala. A mandala is a geometric figure representing the entire universe. It has a natural order and hierarchy. We are aware of and create this harmony. When this harmony is disrupted we feel uneasy. This harmony is described by the principle of La, Nin, and Lu, translated "Heaven, Earth and Man." The human body has this natural hierarchy. Our head and neck form the heaven principle, the torso is the man principle and our legs are the earth principle. We wouldn't wear our shoes on our heads, would we? Can we arrange our homes in this fashion as well? Our entire life begins to be part of the harmony and flows due to our awareness of the natural order of things.

Authentic Presence

Enlightened society is not about destroying the world we have and starting over. It is about fully manifesting who we are, our warriorship and our basic goodness, so that we can help others. It is about shifting the world, one conversation at a time. One drunk helping and another is the fundamental strength of the recovery community. This is how we will help manifest enlightened society. Through our own practice and training we achieve some merit and virtue, which is reflected in our being as authentic presence. Authentic presence brings together meekness, perkiness, and outrageousness to achieve inscrutability. The power of authentic presence comes from our connection to windhorse.

We have all seen people who have this magnificent presence. Confident without arrogance, genuine and caring, these people draw others to them and seem to accomplish things effortlessly. It is not that they accomplish things with little effort; it is that their effort is directed in the right locations and purposes. There are moments, glimpses of this power, that we all experience. We align our body and mind, feel our windhorse and genuineness, and things unfold smoothly and almost effortlessly. The more we can connect and manifest this presence, the more we will connect with others. We will draw them to us and help them to find their own genuineness.

This is the culmination of the twelve steps, a sense of genuineness. You could also use the words worthiness or wholeness. Wholeness is what the Big Book says we are looking for. Wholeness is achieved, according to the Big Book, by filling that hole in our soul with spirituality, with a connection to a power greater than ourselves. This is what draws other people to us, to want what we have. When we have this, there is nothing for drugs or alcohol to fix. We are, as Shantideva describes "like a block of wood," able to withstand the emotional currents of the world. We can ride our windhorse with purpose into the world.

Each of us will have to find our own way to accomplish this wholeness. Each of us will have to figure out how we will help manifest enlightened society. How we help one person will not be what works for the next person. Free from dependence on drugs and alcohol, "we can use our mental faculties with ease" to help others. To serve others. To get off the me plan.

William Alexander in his seminal book *Cool Water* talks about how once we discover a sense of wholeness we are truly recovered from our seemingly hopeless state of mind and body. For him that moment occurred while he was walking along in Plum Village holding Thich Nhat Hanh's hand. Yet we do not need to be walking hand in hand with a great spiritual leader. It can happen to us

Basic Sobriety

through these steps, through our practice and our warriorship. It exists within each of us.

May you find it now.

May these words be of benefit to all in samsara;
  May it help free them from passion, aggression and
    indifference;
  May it help all beings discover the joy and freedom
  of a life free from addiction.
  By this goodness may all be good.

Conclusion

I hope this book causes conversation, discussion and debate. How else can a book about the Twelve Steps and Buddhism be received? When the idea for this book first came to mind, I knew more than I do today, or at least I believed myself more resolutely. Just like a Fourth Step, this is the best I have for this period of my life. Down the road, I will discover entirely new ideas and concepts. This book is the beginning of a discussion that I hope will help others explore their own recovery and spiritual paths.

As an alcoholic, I did not want to wait months for book agents or publishers to get back to me. Therefore this book has been self-published and mostly self-edited as well. If there are any errors, redundancies, formatting errors and the lot they are solely my mistake. This too goes for the dharma and recovery ideas covered in this book. Any error or misrepresentation is my error alone. If there is something you believe should be changed, please contact me at the email address basicsobriety@gmail.com

Getting to this point has been quite a journey. I am grateful for the support and encouragement I received from so many people along the way. To my wife who has allowed me the space to stumble and falter during my process of recovery and yet continues to still love me. To all my children who have forever been imprinted by my life before recovery and after, may the father I am becoming one day erase the father I once was. My sponsorship family as I would not be the man I am today.

To the rest of my family, teachers, fellow travelers and people in recovery, to everyone who sat with me at a Heart of Recovery meeting, you are all in these pages. Your names have been changed to protect the innocent (or guilty) of course, but this book is for you and about you.

Basic Sobriety

Basic Sobriety